How to Live the Christian Life

How to Live the Christian Life

by
James Montgomery Boice

MOODY PRESS

© 1973, 1982 by
THE MOODY BIBLE INSTITUTE
OF CHICAGO

Former title: *How to Really Live It Up*

All rights reserved. No part of this book may be reproduced in any form without permission in writing from the publisher, except in the case of brief quotations embodied in critical articles or reviews.

All Scripture quotations, except those noted otherwise, are from the *New American Standard Bible*, © 1960, 1962, 1964, 1968, 1971, 1972, 1973, 1975, and 1977 by The Lockman Foundation, and are used by permission.

Library of Congress Cataloging in Publication Data

Boice, James Montgomery, 1938-
   How to live the Christian life.
   Reprint. Originally published: How to really live it up. Grand Rapids, Mich.: Zondervan Pub. House, 1973.
   Includes bibliographical references and indexes. 1. Christian life—Presbyterian authors. I. Title.
BV4501.2.B615   1982   248.4'851   81-18839
ISBN 0-8024-3666-8   AACR2

2 3 4 5 6 7 Printing/LC/Year 87 86 85 84 83 82

Printed in the United States of America

Contents

CHAPTER		PAGE
	Preface	7
1.	How to Become a Christian	9
2.	How to Pray	17
3.	How to Worship God	25
4.	How to Know the Will of God	33
5.	How to Know God's Will in Doubtful Situations	43
6.	How to Get Along With Other Christians	51
7.	How to Have a Happy Marriage	57
8.	How to Be Happy as a Family	65
9.	How to Defeat Temptation	75
10.	How to Overcome Anger	83
11.	How to Be Free From Worry	89
12.	How to Triumph in Suffering	97
13.	How to Tell Others About Christ	105
	Scripture Index	113
	Subject Index	115

To Him
*who of God is made unto us
wisdom, and righteousness, and
sanctification, and redemption*

Preface

The chapters that appear in this book are practical studies of practical matters. They are not intended to be profound, though I trust that in places they do reflect the profundity of the Word of God. They are merely designed to be helpful. They are attempts to bring the clear and most basic principles of the Bible to bear on problems that each of us faces at some period or another in his life: How do I become a Christian? How can I know the will of God? How can I overcome anger, worry, or temptation? How can I tell others about Jesus Christ?

I am aware that these studies will not answer all the questions that everyone who reads them may have, but they should be a help to most people in at least some of their difficulties.

The studies themselves are an offshoot of the ministry of The Bible Study Hour, in which I have had the privilege of participating for many years. Many of my weekly radio messages seemed to the staff to lend themselves to an overall "how-to" theme. So with some alterations they were offered over the air as a series of "how-to" booklets. Then they were prepared as a special collection of fifteen-minute radio broadcasts that were aired on many stations across the country. The response to the series has been so good that the studies are now being issued in this book—together for the first time.

It is my prayer and desire that this book, to the degree that it is faithful to the great principles of the Word of God and is blessed by the Holy Spirit, will help many to find the path of upward growth and progress as they seek to live the Christian life.

JAMES MONTGOMERY BOICE

1
How to Become a Christian

Some time ago a young man said to me that "How to become a Christian" is the best-kept secret in America. I believe he was right. The answer to the question "How can I become a Christian?" or "How can I get right with God?" is not often clearly stated in our pulpits, and lay Christians are not always able to give an answer either. As a result, many people are filled with a false confidence before God—because of biblical knowledge, good works, optimism, or whatever it might be. And others are simply indifferent or confused.

How does a person become a Christian? People have come to faith by various roads, of course. Nevertheless, at the heart of the matter—when Christianity is boiled down to its bare essentials—the answer is always the same and is quite simple. There are three points: two things we must believe and one thing we must do. They are simple as ABC. *A* stands for "admit." We must admit that we are less perfect than God and that we should, therefore, be separated from His presence forever. *B* stands for "believe." We must believe that God loves us in spite of our sin and that He has acted in Jesus Christ to remove sin and restore us to Himself. *C* stands for "commit." That is the final act of the will by which we give up trying to run our own lives and instead place ourselves in the hands of Jesus, who died for us and rose again.

First, God demands that we admit without reservation that we are less perfect than He is and that we should, therefore, be separated from His presence forever. God is perfect, and anyone who fails to meet that standard deserves to be separated from Him.

It is difficult for the non-Christian to accept that principle. But it should not be, for we recognize the principle in many things that are accepted naturally. Take medicine for an example. No one would question the right of a state to make the requirements for the practice of medicine as high as is reasonably possible. If you want to be a doctor, you must meet these requirements. You must first graduate from college with a Bachelor of Science or a Bachelor of Arts degree. After that you must graduate from medical school with an M.D. degree. This must be followed by a one-year internship under the supervision of competent doctors. Then you must pass an examination which leads to licensing by the state. No sane person would trust himself to a man who claims to be able to practice medicine but has not passed these requirements.

In the same way, God has a right to His requirements. They are summed up as perfection. The only difference between this demand and the demands of the state boards of medicine is that no one has ever met God's standards. No one ever will. God says, "For all have sinned and fall short of the glory of God" (Romans 3:23). Consequently, men deserve separation from God as surely as quacks should be barred from the medical profession.

Sometimes people object to that teaching of the Word of God because they think that somehow it makes them the same as the worst criminals. In one sense, of course, it does, for both equally need a Savior. Yet that confuses the point. I will admit that if you are a fine person with good character, I would much rather have you than a scoundrel for a friend. However, it is not a question of what satisfies me but what satisfies God. Human goodness is not good enough for God. And that means that although it will see a man through this life, often with flying colors, it will not see him to heaven.

There are several reasons for that. First, man's righteousness is not righteousness from God's point of view. Righteousness is one of those things, like perfection or wholeness, that loses its meaning entirely if you divide it. Perfection is a whole. You cannot be half perfect. To be half perfect is to be imperfect; it is not perfection at all. You cannot have a "whole" half of an orange. You either have a whole orange or you have part of an orange. Righteousness is exactly the same. You are either completely righteous by God's definition, or you are not righteous at all. Thus Jesus taught, in what is undoubtedly the most important verse in the Sermon on the Mount, "Therefore you are to be perfect, as your heavenly Father is perfect" (Matthew 5:48). That is the standard. All men fall short of it, and falling short of it, they miss it all.

If you have a boat tied up to a dock by a chain that has ten links in it, how many links do you have to break in order to set it adrift? Just one! And if there is a churning cataract fifty yards downriver, the boat will go over it and be destroyed just as easily with one link broken as with all ten broken. It is the same spiritually. Some men break all the links of God's law, and we call them criminals. We put them in prison if we catch them. Other people carefully pry open just one of the links, and we try to overlook it since all of us are at least that guilty. But we are all adrift and headed toward the cataract. That is what is meant when we say that all men are equally unrighteous from God's point of view.

Second, the righteousness of which men are so proud is an external righteousness. To a certain extent we can pull ourselves up by our own bootstraps morally. If you are an alcoholic, you can discipline yourself to attend meetings of Alcoholics Anonymous and get rid of the habit of drink. You can get control of yourself and enter into a useful life. People will even admire you for having overcome your problem. But although you can do all that outwardly, you cannot do anything about your inner nature. You can be scrupulous in the affairs of your life, so that you are not the least bit dishonest in business. But you cannot make your heart loving if your heart is not loving. You cannot make yourself humble if you are not humble. You cannot make yourself pure. Hence, the second reason why human righteousness will not get anywhere with God is that the only righteousness of which we are capable is external. That in itself produces hopelessness, for God demands a transformation of the heart.

Third, the pursuit of human goodness blinds men to their true condition. I remember seeing a movie years ago in which a number of men in canoes were racing each other on a river. They were paddling as fast as they could go. First one man would get ahead; then another man would get ahead. But the irony of the movie was that the water was moving down the stream faster than their boats were moving up. So, although they were racing one another as fast as their paddles could take them, all the while they were being swept toward a waterfall. In the final scene all the boats went over the waterfall together.

That is what men are doing. They have their minds so much on themselves they do not see that the goodness of which they are capable is not taking them anywhere.

In the early part of this century there was a well-known gangster in New York named Two-Gun Crowley. Two-Gun Crowley was the kind of person who killed without any apparent qualms. One day when he was parked by the side of the road a policeman walked up to his car and asked to see his license. Instead of producing it, Crowley pulled out a gun and shot the policeman. As the officer lay prostrate on the ground, Crowley leaped from his car, took the officer's gun, and fired five more shots into his body. That's the kind of man he was. The time came, however, when the police cornered Crowley in his girl friend's apartment in one of the more fashionable districts of the city. Crowley was captured and sent to Sing Sing Prison.

Now you might ask, "What did a man like that think of

himself?" Surely he must have known what he was like. He must have said, "I am a bad man; I kill people." But that was not the case. The bloodstained note he wrote while shooting it out with the police reads, "Under my coat is a weary heart, but a kind one—one that would do nobody any harm." Later, when he was sitting on death row waiting to be executed, did he say, "This is what I get for killing policemen"? No! What he said was, "This is what I get for defending myself."

Another man once said, "I have spent the best years of my life giving people the lighter pleasures, and all I get is abuse, the existence of a hunted man." The man speaking was Al Capone, one of the most notorious gangsters of the Chicago gangland era.

The point is this. If men like Two-Gun Crowley and Al Capone did not recognize the evil in their characters, how much less do the so-called moral people of our society recognize their own evil. And yet, from God's perspective, they need to see it. So, the third reason why God will not deal in human goodness is that it blinds men to their true condition.

Fourth, human righteousness is actually a different kind of righteousness from that which God demands. God asks for divine righteousness, and human righteousness is not divine at all.

That is hard to understand, but the following illustration may help. The accumulation of human righteousness is like playing the game of Monopoly®. The object of the game is to collect as much money and property as one can. The game is enjoyable, but only a fool would take his Monopoly® earnings and go into town to buy groceries. Monopoly® is a game; a different currency is used in the real world. It is the same spiritually. Yet there are people who think they are collecting assets before God, when they are only collecting human righteousness. God tells us that we must leave the play currency to deal in His currency—His goodness. Man's goodness has no real value in heaven.

The second truth that God asks you to believe if you are to become a Christian is that He loves you in spite of your sin and that He has acted in Jesus Christ to remove that sin and to begin to make you perfect once more by conforming you to Christ's image. That is the heart of such scripture passages as John 3:16 and Romans 5:8. Romans 5:8 says, "But God demonstrates His own love toward us, in that while we were yet sinners, Christ died for us." John 3:16 says, "For God so loved the world, that He gave His only begotten Son, that whoever believes in Him should not perish, but have eternal life."

There are two parts to this transaction. On the one hand, we are sinners and sin must be punished. God says that Christ died to bear that punishment. The second part is that, on the basis of Christ's death, God now comes to us and offers us His own righteousness, divine righteousness, entirely as a free gift. Before, we were clothed in sin; now we are clothed in righteousness. Before, we were no people; now we are God's people. Before, we were aliens; now we are citizens of heaven. Before, we were separated from God; now we have fellowship with God, and our life here and now is transformed by His presence.

Many years ago there was a Pharisee who found that those first two points were indeed true and who experienced a transformation of his life as a result. He is probably the best-known rabbi that ever lived. His name is Paul. In his youth Paul had gloried in his achievement as a Pharisee. He felt he had achieved everything. Yet, near the end of his life, when he looked back to add it all up, he recognized that all he had achieved came to nothing and the only thing that counted was Christ.

Before that happened, Paul thought he had attained to righteousness by keeping *his* concept of God's law. Afterward he knew that all his own righteousness was as filthy rags in God's sight. He had once said, "As to the righteousness which is in the Law, [I am] found blameless" (Philippians 3:6). Now he said he was the chief of sinners (1 Timothy 1:15).

When Paul met Christ, he came to know what righteousness was. As he looked at his own supposed goodness in the white light of God's righteousness, his goodness seemed filthy. He had no other word for it but *rubbish*. He crossed it all out. All the

How to Become a Christian

things he had considered assets he moved over into the column of liabilities, because, he said, "These things have actually kept me from God's righteousness." Under the column of assets he wrote, "Jesus Christ alone."

Are you trusting in the kind of goodness that will never be accepted by God? If you are, you must learn that your goodness will keep you from God. However, if you lay your goodness aside, counting it loss, God will credit to your account Jesus Christ, "who became to us wisdom from God, and righteousness and sanctification, and redemption" (1 Corinthians 1:30).

The third demand is that there must be an act by which you commit yourself to Christ. Or, to put it another way, you must open the gate of your heart and admit Him. That does not mean that you are responsible for your own salvation. If you do open the door, it is only because Christ is there beforehand moving you to do it. And yet, from your own point of view, the act itself is absolutely indispensable.

C. S. Lewis, the great Christian apologist, in his book *Surprised by Joy*, wrote of his own personal conversion:

> "I was going up Headington Hill on the top of a bus. Without words and (I think) almost without images, a fact about myself was somehow presented to me. I became aware that I was holding something at bay, or shutting something out. Or, if you like, that I was wearing some stiff clothing, like corsets, or even a suit of armor, as if I were a lobster. I felt myself being, there and then, given a free choice. I could open the door or keep it shut; I could unbuckle the armor or keep it on. Neither choice was presented as a duty; no threat or promise was attached to either, though I knew that to open the door or to take off the corset meant the incalculable. The choice appeared to be momentous but it was also strangely unemotional. I was moved by no desires or fears. In a sense I was not moved by anything. I chose to open, to unbuckle, to loosen the rein. I say, 'I chose,' yet it did not really seem possible to do the opposite."

Later, in his room at Magdalen College in Cambridge, Lewis made the final decision. "In the Trinity Term of 1929 I gave in, and admitted that God was God, and knelt and prayed: perhaps, that night, the most dejected and reluctant convert in all England."[1]

It does not matter in the slightest whether you feel the dejection of Lewis, the peace Martin Luther felt, or the joy experienced by countless others. What matters is the reality of your own personal commitment to Jesus. Are you a Christian? That is the question. Is it real? The answer does not depend upon your good works but rather upon your relationship to the Savior. Have you ever asked Jesus Christ to be your Savior? You must say something like, "Lord Jesus Christ, I *admit* that I am less perfect than You are and, therefore, that I deserve nothing—that I have no claims upon You. Nevertheless, I *believe* that You love me and died for me and that now by grace I can stand before You, clothed in Your righteousness. I *commit* my life to You. Receive me now as one of Your followers."

This has been the heart of Christian experience. It has been embodied in many of our hymns. One of them says:

> Nothing in my hand I bring,
> Simply to thy cross I cling;
> Naked, come to thee for dress;
> Helpless, look to thee for grace;
> Foul, I to the fountain fly;
> Wash me, Savior, or I die.
> Rock of ages, cleft for me,
> Let me hide myself in thee.

If you pray that prayer, God will wash you, God will cleanse you. And He will give you that righteousness that is above anything that man can attain.

Notes

1. C. S. Lewis, *Surprised by Joy* (New York: Harcourt, Brace & World, 1955), pp. 224, 228-29.

2
How to Pray

Perhaps you have met some Christians who believe that it is hardly necessary to pray. They may tell you that everything is in God's hands, that He does what He wants to do whether or not you pray about it. On the other hand, you may have met others who tell you that almost everything is contingent upon prayer and that God will do very little unless you ask for it.

Probably you are somewhere in between. No doubt you believe that God is indeed in charge of things and is accomplishing His own purposes, but you also believe that He responds to your prayers and, in fact, even urges you to pray to Him. Unfortunately, you may be confused and uncertain about prayer. You wonder how you should pray, what you should pray for, and sometimes whether you should even pray at all.

I have heard people say things like this: "I don't pray much because I don't go to church much. A person should be in church to pray." "Prayer is for weak, insecure people." "I pray when I'm desperate." People ask me when they should pray and how they should pray. Sometimes they even ask, "Why should I pray?"

Many of those questions are answered when we realize that prayer is basically talking with God. Therefore it should be as natural for us to pray as for a child to come to his parents for guidance, consolation, help, or merely sharing the day's experiences. If you are a child of God—as the Bible says you are, if you have admitted that you are a sinner, believed on the Lord Jesus Christ as your Savior, and committed yourself to Him—there need be no restrictions on the time, place, and manner in which you speak to Him.

All those questions about prayer were also raised in Christ's day, of course. So when Jesus began to teach about prayer He dealt with them—sometimes by direct teaching and at other times by example, as in the Lord's Prayer.

In one of His most helpful teachings about prayer, Jesus said,

> When you pray, you are not to be as the hypocrites; for they love to stand and pray in the synagogues and on the street corners, in order to be seen by men. Truly I say to you, they have their reward in full.
>
> But you, when you pray, go into your inner room, and when you have shut your door, pray to your Father who is in secret, and your Father who sees in secret will repay you.
>
> And when you are praying, do not use meaningless repetition, as the Gentiles do, for they suppose that they will be heard for their many words.
>
> Therefore do not be like them; for your Father knows what you need, before you ask Him (Matthew 6:5-8).

I must admit that those verses have often been taken as teaching the very opposite of what I have been saying: that is, as teaching that there *are* restrictions on prayer. Some persons have understood them to teach that there is to be no such thing as public prayer. But that is foolish, because both the disciples and Jesus Himself prayed publicly. Some have said that there is to be no such thing as prayer with others, no prayer meetings. That is nonsense, too, and the practice of Jesus and the early Christians refutes that notion.

Actually, those verses are concerned with the tendency of all men to pray to themselves and to other persons rather than to God. They teach that prayer must always be made to God and that, as a consequence, it must be made in the knowledge that God is always more ready to answer than we are to pray to Him. Let me make this the first great principle of true prayer. True prayer is *prayer that is offered to God, our heavenly Father.*

Perhaps you are saying, "But isn't that obvious? Aren't all prayers offered to God?" I don't think so. And I don't think that it is obvious. All prayers are *not* offered to God, otherwise Jesus would not have made a point of stressing that they should be.

You may reply, "Oh, I think I know what you mean. You are referring to the prayers of the heathen, those that are offered to idols." Well, partially, but there are other prayers that are not offered to God.

You say, "Oh, you must mean prayers to the saints." Yes, that too. But not only that. Actually, I would not be surprised if God told us that not one prayer in a hundred of those that fill our churches on a typical Sunday morning is actually made to Him—to the Almighty God, the Father of the Lord Jesus Christ. Isn't it true that our prayers are often made to men or to the one praying?

Years ago a minister from New England described an ornate and elaborate prayer in a fashionable Boston church as "the most eloquent prayer ever offered to a Boston audience." That was perceptive, for he meant that the person who prayed was much more concerned with impressing his listeners than with approaching God.

Do your prayers bring you into the presence of God, or do they make you like the Boston preacher? Perhaps most of the time when you pray you are really thinking far more of your friends, your busy schedule, or what you are asking for than you are of the great God whom you are approaching and of whom you are asking it.

I am convinced that if a person really learns to pray *to God,* and not to other people or to himself, prayer will necessarily become real and exciting for him. It will no longer be a farce.

And many of the questions he might ask—"Where should I pray?" "How should I pray?" and "When should I pray?"—will not even occur to him.

In one of his books Reuben A. Torrey, the great Bible teacher and evangelist, told of the difficulty he used to have in prayer and how that changed when he suddenly realized that prayer was essentially conversation with God. He wrote: "The day came when I realized what real prayer meant, realized that prayer was having an audience with God, actually coming into the presence of God and asking and getting things from Him. And the realization of that fact transformed my prayer life. Before that, prayer had been a mere duty, and sometimes a very irksome duty, but from that time on prayer has been not merely a duty but a privilege, one of the most highly esteemed privileges of life. Before that the thought I had was, 'How much time must I spend in prayer?' The thought that now possesses me is, 'How much time may I spend in prayer without neglecting the other privileges and duties of life?' "[1]

Perhaps you have another question at this point. For, if it is true that prayer is communing with God, the question naturally comes up about the means of access to Him. How can a sinful human being approach a God who is holy? Is it even possible? And if it is, what does it mean in terms of the way that we can approach Him?

The answer to that question brings us to the second great principle of prayer. True prayer is *prayer offered to God the Father on the basis of the death of Jesus Christ, his Son.* The author of the book of Hebrews put it like this: "Since therefore, brethren, we have confidence to enter the holy place by the blood of Jesus ... let us draw near with a sincere heart in full assurance of faith" (Hebrews 10:19, 22). Jesus taught the same principle when He said, "I am the way, and the truth, and the life; no one comes to the Father, but through Me" (John 14:6).

What does that mean? First, it means that if you were to approach God as you are, apart from Jesus Christ, God would have to turn from you. God is holy. And if He is to be true to His

How to Pray

Word and to His nature, He must turn from all that is unholy and imperfect. If it were not for Jesus Christ, God would have had to turn a deaf ear to every prayer offered by every human being.

However, God also tells you that anyone can be purified in His sight through faith in the death of Jesus Christ and that in that state you may come. In fact, you are even urged to come.

The best person in this world is unable to come into the presence of God on the basis of any merit of his own. He cannot receive anything from God on the grounds of his own goodness. Yet, on the ground of the shed blood of Jesus Christ, the worst sinner who ever walked on the face of this earth, who has turned from his sin and accepted Jesus Christ as his Savior, can come any day of the year, at any hour of the day or night, at any place, and with boldness can speak out of the longing of his heart and get from God what he asks.

Second, the fact that you come to God through Christ means that you can come without guilt. One of my friends says he believes guilt is the major culprit in keeping people from praying. I believe he is right. People do feel guilty before God. They feel ashamed and unqualified to ask anything from Him. There are good reasons for that guilt, too. But the fact that you come through Jesus Christ means that you come as one whose guilt is removed. Yes, you are a sinner; but the sin has been dealt with. Now you stand as a righteous person before God.

The third consequence of coming through the Lord Jesus Christ is that you come thankfully and joyfully. You do not come as a slave to his master, begging. You come as one who has already received so much from God's hands that your uppermost thought should be one of gratitude, joy, and thanksgiving.

Years ago someone pointed out to me that the word *acts* can be used as an acrostic to remind us of the important elements in praying. *A* stands for "adoration." Adoration comes first if you are really approaching God. *C* is for "confession," for once you have praised God, you will want to confess sin in those areas where you have offended Him. *T* is for "thanksgiving." *S* is for "supplications." Our supplications or requests quite naturally come last and should include requests for the needs of others, as well as for those things that we need personally.

True prayer is, therefore, prayer to God the Father through the Lord Jesus Christ.

But prayer is one thing more. It is also *in the Holy Spirit*. That is the third great principle of prayer. Ephesians 2:18 says of the Jews and Gentiles, "For through Him [that is, through Jesus Christ] we both have our access *in one Spirit* to the Father" (italics added).

That verse, of course, reinforces the truth we have just been considering, for it says that prayer is to be made through the Lord Jesus Christ. But that is not the only idea in the verse. It also says that prayer is to be made in the Holy Spirit. It is the work of the Holy Spirit to lead you into God's presence, to point God out to you, and thus to make God real when you pray. Perhaps I can point that up by the underlying meaning of the word *access*. The Greek word that lies behind our English translation is *prosagoge*, which literally means "an introduction." The Holy Spirit introduces you to God. Thus, the Holy Spirit makes God real to you while, at the same time, instructing you as to how you should pray (Romans 8:26-27).

Have you ever begun to pray and felt that God was far away and unreal? If you have, one of two things may be wrong. First, it may be that sin or disobedience to God is hindering you. The Bible records David as saying, "If I regard wickedness in my heart, the Lord will not hear" (Psalm 66:18). If that is the case, you need to confess the sin openly.

It may also be the case, however, that other things are filling your mind or that worries are obscuring the sense you should have of God's presence. What are you to do in that case? Should you stop and pray some other time? Certainly not, for you probably need prayer most at that moment. Instead of not praying, you should only be still and, looking to God, ask Him to work through His Holy Spirit to make Himself real to you and to lead you into His presence. Many Christians find that their most wonderful times of prayer are those in which they start without a clear sense of God's presence but come to it fully by praying.

All this is really only an amplification of the first part of Jesus' instruction about prayer in the Sermon on the Mount. But there is a second part also. It is the part in which Jesus teaches that God is more willing to answer your prayers than you are to pray and that, as a result, the Christian who prays in God's will can pray with great confidence. Jesus said, "And when you are praying, do not use meaningless repetition, as the Gentiles do, for they suppose that they will be heard for their many words. Therefore do not be like them; for your Father knows what you need, before you ask Him" (Matthew 6:7-8).

There is a great deal involved in that, of course, for it certainly does not mean that God will grant any stupid thing you ask for. If you are to receive the things you ask for, you must have a knowledge of God's will and God's ways. Those are given to you only through Scripture.

One of the greatest verses on prayer in the Bible is 1 John 3:22: "And whatever we ask we receive from Him, because we keep His commandments and do the things that are pleasing in His sight." That remarkable statement is totally in keeping with Jesus' teaching in the Sermon on the Mount. John said that his prayers were always answered and that he had full confidence that they would always continue to be answered.

It is so remarkable that we cannot help but ask, "John, how can you make such a statement? Our prayers are not always answered (or do not seem to be answered). And yet you say that you always receive that for which you ask."

"Well," John would say, "just read the verse more carefully. I say that I receive the things that I request, but I also say why. It is because I keep His commandments and do those things that are pleasing in His sight. Do you do that? If you do, then you, too, will receive the things you ask for."

It was a sense of having kept God's commandments and doing that which was pleasing to him that gave Luther his boldness in prayer. In 1540 Luther's great friend and assistant, Frederick

Myconius, became sick and was expected to die within a short time. On his bed he wrote a loving farewell note to Luther with a trembling hand. Luther received the letter and instantly sent back a reply: "I command thee in the name of God to live because I still have need of thee in the work of reforming the church. . . . The Lord will never let me hear that thou art dead, but will permit thee to survive me. For this I am praying, this is my will, and may my will be done, because I seek only to glorify the name of God."

Those words are almost shocking to us, since we live in a more sensitive and cautious day, but they were certainly from God. For, although Myconius had already lost the ability to speak when Luther's letter came, in a short time he revived. He recovered completely, and he lived six more years to survive Luther himself by two months.

You are never so relaxed or bold in prayer as when you can look into the face of God and say, "My Father, I do not pray for myself in this thing, and I do not want my will done. I want Your name to be glorified. I ask You to glorify it now in my situation, in my life, and do it in such a way that all men will know it is of You. Amen."

NOTES

1. R. A. Torrey, *The Power of Prayer* (Grand Rapids: Zondervan, 1955), p. 77.

3
How to Worship God

"Christian worship is the most momentous, the most urgent, the most glorious action that can take place in human life."

Those words by the noted Swiss theologian Karl Barth undoubtedly find an echo in the hearts of all who truly know God and earnestly desire to serve Him, regardless of their opinion of Barth's theology. But in spite of the obvious truth that the worship of God is an important and even urgent imperative for Christians, it is a sad fact that in our day much that passes for worship is not worship at all. And many who sincerely desire to worship do not always know how to go about it or where to begin. "What is worship anyway?" they ask. "Who can worship? Where can one worship? How does one worship?"

It is my experience that few books or sermons ever attempt to deal with those questions directly, and even fewer are helpful or of lasting value.

One Bible student has written: "Thanks to our splendid Bible societies and to other effective agencies for the dissemination of the Word, there are today many millions of people who hold 'right opinions,' probably more than ever before in the history of the Church. Yet I wonder if there was ever a time when true spiritual worship was at a lower ebb. To great sections of the Church the art of worship has been lost entirely, and in its place has come that strange and foreign thing called the 'program.' This word has been borrowed from the stage and applied with sad wisdom to the type of public service which now passes for worship among us."[1]

Are those words true, even in part? Are the questions I have just repeated genuine? If so, there is an answer for them all in the words of Jesus. Jesus said, "But an hour is coming, and now is, when the true worshipers shall worship the Father in spirit and truth; for such people the Father seeks to be His worshipers. God is spirit, and those who worship Him must worship in spirit and truth" (John 4:23-24).

Before we begin to look at those words in detail, however, we must first see that worship itself is an important subject and that these are important verses for dealing with it. In Philippians 3:3 the apostle Paul spoke of worship as one of the three great marks that reveal the presence of the new nature within the Christian. He wrote: "For we are the true circumcision, who worship in the Spirit of God and glory in Christ Jesus and put no confidence in the flesh." Most Christians would quickly acknowledge the last point, which is a matter of holding to the true gospel. Many would also think highly of the second point, for joy is important. It is a mark of the Spirit, according to Galatians 5. I strongly suspect, however, that not many think of the worship of God as a mark of the presence of the new nature within. And yet, in this verse it is included along with the two other essentials.

Another way of making this point is to note that there are three great "musts" in John's gospel. The first occurs in chapter 3, verse 7 where Jesus said, "You *must* be born again." The second is in verse 14 of the same chapter: "even so *must* the Son of Man be lifted up." The verses we are studying give us the third "must," for they say that all who worship God "*must* worship Him in spirit and truth." Those three doctrines—the necessity for the new birth, the necessity of Christ's death, and the necessity of true worship—belong together.

Well, then, what is worship? Part of the answer is to be seen in the fact that if you and I had been living in England during the days of the early formation of the English language, between the period of Geoffrey Chaucer and William Shakespeare, we would not have used the word *worship* at all. We would have said, "worth-ship," and we would have meant that in worshiping God we were assigning to God His true worth. Linguistically speaking, that is the same thing as "praising" God or "glorifying" His name.

If we should ask the two most important questions that follow from that definition, however—namely, "What is God's true worth?" and "How do we become aware of it?" we are immediately brought to the heart of Christ's words to the Samaritan woman. For Jesus said that those who acknowledge God's true worth must do so "in spirit and truth." In other words, we must do so "in truth" because truth has to do with what His nature is. And we must do so "in spirit" because only spiritually can we apprehend God's true worth.

Let me explain that a bit further. Many persons have been led astray in thinking that when Jesus spoke of "spirit" in this verse, He was referring to the Holy Spirit. I do not believe that is the case here. There is a sense, of course, in which we only come to worship God after the Holy Spirit has been at work in our hearts, moving us to do so. But in this verse Jesus was not speaking of that. He was speaking of spirit generally, without the definite article, not the Holy Spirit. He was teaching that in the age which He would inaugurate by His death and resurrection, the place of worship would not matter, for a person would not worship merely by being in the right place and doing certain right things. He would worship in his spirit, which could be anywhere.

I believe that I can make that even clearer by placing it in the context of the three parts of man's nature. Man is a trinity. He has a body, a soul, and a spirit. Jesus was saying that nothing is true worship of God except what takes place in man's spirit.

Many people worship with the body. They consider themselves to have worshiped if they have been in the right place doing the right things at the right time. The woman at the well thought that meant being either at the Temple in Jerusalem or on Mount Gerizim at the Samaritans' temple. In our day the reference would be to people who think they have worshiped God simply because they have occupied a seat in a church on Sunday morning, sung a hymn, lit a candle, crossed themselves, or knelt in the aisle. Jesus said that is not worship. Those customs may be vehicles for real worship. In some cases they may also hinder it. But they are not worship in themselves. Therefore, we must not confuse worship with the partciular things we do on Sunday morning.

In addition, however, we must not confuse worship with feelings, for worship does not originate with the soul either, any more than it originates with the body. The soul is the seat of our emotions. It may be the case, and often is, that the emotions are stirred in real worship. At times tears fill the eyes or joy floods the heart. But, unfortunately, it is possible for those things to happen without worship being present. It is possible to be moved by a song or by oratory and yet not come to a genuine awareness of God and a fuller praise of His ways and nature.

True worship occurs only when man's spirit, that part of him that is akin to the divine nature (for God is spirit), actually meets with God, praising Him for His love, wisdom, beauty, truth, holiness, compassion, mercy, grace, power, and all His other attributes. William Barclay has written on this point, "The true, the genuine worship is when man, through his spirit, attains to friendship and intimacy with God. True and genuine worship is not to come to a certain place; it is not to go through a certain ritual or liturgy; it is not even to bring certain gifts. True worship is when the spirit, the immortal and invisible part of man, speaks to and meets with God, who is immortal and invisible."²

Incidentally, the truth that we are to worship God in spirit also has bearing upon the question of the various types of liturgy used in Christian churches. For it means that, with the exception of liturgical elements that suggest wrong doctrine, there is no liturgy that is inherently better or worse than any other. For any given congregation, one type of service will presumably be more valuable than another. But the decision as to what that type of service should be is to be arrived at, not by asking whether one likes emotional or nonemotional hymns, extemporaneous or read prayers, congregational responses or silence—in short, whether one prefers Anglican, Lutheran, Presbyterian, Methodist, Baptist, Congregational, or Quaker liturgies, but by asking how effective the service is in turning the attention of the worshiper away from the service itself to God. In that respect, an order of worship is to be evaluated on the same basis as we are to evaluate the preacher.

In thinking through this particular issue, I have been greatly helped by the concepts of C. S. Lewis. Lewis was a member of the Church of England and was accustomed to various forms of what we generally call a "liturgical" service. Nevertheless, Lewis did not plead for liturgy. He asked merely for uniformity, on the grounds that novelty in the worship service at best turns our attention to the novelty and at the worst turns it to the one who is enacting the liturgy.

Lewis wrote, "As long as you notice, and have to count the steps, you are not yet dancing but only learning to dance. A good shoe is a shoe you don't notice. Good reading becomes possible when you need not consciously think about eyes, or light, or print, or spelling. The perfect church service would be one we were almost unaware of; our attention would have been on God."³ We should pray that God will use any form of church service in which we happen to be participating to that end.

Finally, we need to notice that the true worship of God is a worship not only in spirit but in truth. What does that mean? What does it mean to worship God "in truth"?

First, it means that we must approach God truthfully, that is, *honestly* or *wholeheartedly*. That is what Jesus was referring to in a negative way when he said of the people of His day, "This people honors Me with their lips, but their heart is far away from Me. But in vain do they worship Me" (Matthew 15:8-9). According to Jesus, no worship is true worship unless there is an honesty of heart on the part of the worshiper. We must not pretend to worship. We must worship honestly, knowing that our hearts are open books before God.

Second, we must worship on the basis of the *biblical revelation*. That is also implied in the verses I have just quoted. For the verse that begins "In vain do they worship Me" goes on to condemn those who have substituted "the doctrines of men" for the doctrines of Scripture. "Thy word is truth," says the Scripture (John 17:17). So if we are to worship "in truth," as God commanded us to do, our worship must be in accord with the principles and admonitions of that Book.

When the Protestant Reformation first took place under Martin Luther in the early sixteenth century, and the doctrines and principles of the Word of God, long covered over by the traditions and encrustations of medieval church ceremony, again came into prominence, there was an immediate elevation of the Word of God in Protestant services. Calvin particularly carried that out with thoroughness, ordering that the altars (long the center of the Mass) be removed from the churches and that a pulpit with a Bible upon it be placed in the center of the building. That was not to be at the side of the room, but in the very center, where every line of the architecture would carry the gaze of the worshiper to the Book that alone contains the way of salvation and outlines the principles upon which the church of the living God is to be governed.

Finally, to approach God "in truth" means that we must approach God *Christocentrically*. That means "in Christ," for that is God's way of approach to Him. Jesus Himself signified this

How to Worship God

when He said to His disciples, "I am the way, and the truth, and the life; no one comes to the Father, but through Me" (John 14:6). That is a difficult point for many to accept, of course. But that is precisely why God has taken such pains to teach that Jesus is the way of approach to Him. We see that even in the Old Testament in the instructions given to Moses for the design of the tabernacle.

What was the original tabernacle? It was not a thing of great beauty or permanence. It had no stained-glass windows, no great arches. It was made of pieces of wood and animal skins. But every part of it was significant. The tabernacle taught the way to God. Take that tabernacle with its altar for sacrifice, its laver for cleansing, its Holy Place and its Holy of Holies, and you have a perfect illustration of how a person must approach God. The altar, which is the first thing we come to, is the cross of Christ. It was given to teach that without the shedding of blood there is no remission of sins and to direct attention to the Lamb of God who would come to take away the sin of the world. The laver, which comes next, is a picture of cleansing that Christ provides when we confess our sins and enter into fellowship with Him. The table of shewbread, which was within the Holy Place, speaks of Christ as the bread of life. The altar of incense is a picture of prayer, for we grow by prayer as well as by feeding on Christ in Bible study. Behind the altar of incense was the great veil, dividing the Holy Place from the Holy of Holies. This veil was torn in two at the moment of Christ's death to demonstrate that His death was the fulfillment of all those figures and the basis of the fullness of approach to the Almighty. Finally, within the Holy of Holies was the Ark of the covenant with the Mercy Seat upon which the high priest placed the blood of the lamb on the Day of Atonement. There, symbolized by the space above the Mercy Seat, was the presence of God. We can now come into His presence because of His great mercy revealed in the death of Christ for us.

There is no other way to come to God. To come through Christ—the Christ of the altar, laver, shewbread, incense, veil, and Mercy Seat—is to come in truth. He is the truth. We must come in God's way and not in any way of human devising.

What way are we to come? We are to come *honestly*, that is, without hypocrisy. We are to come *biblically*. And we are to come *focusing on Jesus Christ*. In that way, we will attain to friendship with God and be awakened to His glory, which is the essence of worship.

The wonder of Christian worship is that, when we come to God in that way, we find Him inexhaustible and discover that our desire to know and worship Him further is increased. Bernard of Clairvaux is one who knew that. He wrote toward the middle of the twelfth century:

> Jesus, thou joy of loving hearts,
> Thou Fount of life, thou Light of men,
> From the best bliss that earth imparts,
> We turn unfilled to thee again.
>
> We taste thee, O thou living Bread!
> And long to feast upon thee still;
> We drink of thee, the fountainhead,
> And thirst our souls from thee to fill.

When we so come, when we worship in that way, we find ourselves approaching what the compilers of the Westminster Shorter Catechism rightly described as the chief end of man. The first question of the catechism asks, "What is the chief end of man?" And the answer is, "Man's chief end is to glorify God, and to enjoy Him forever."

NOTES

1. From A. W. Tozer, *The Pursuit of God* (Harrisburg, Pa.: Christian Publications, 1948), p. 9.
2. William Barclay, ed., *The Gospel of John*, 2 vols. (Philadelphia: Westminster, 1958), 1:154.
3. C. S. Lewis, *Letters to Malcolm: Chiefly on Prayer* (New York: Harcourt, Brace & World, 1964), p. 4.

4

How to Know the Will of God

How can you know God's will? How is it possible for you to know the mind of God? If God has a plan for your life, how does He reveal it to you? How can you find that plan? How does a sinful, finite human being come to know what a holy and infinite God desires? In this chapter we are going to be looking at verses that assure us that God will give us the guidance we need for every aspect of our lives and that show us how to find that guidance.

A pilot once explained to me how airplanes are kept on their courses by radar. A pilot cannot always see what is coming, particularly in bad weather. At best he can see only about a hundred miles. And yet he can fly an aircraft safely in all kinds of weather, for the course is marked out for him by radar. If he deviates either to the right or to the left, the radar warns him accordingly. God guides us in the same way. The verses we are going to be looking at do not mean that we will always be able to see more than one step ahead in our Christian lives. They do not mean that we will always be able to see ahead at all. But they do mean that God has a plan for our lives and that He will reveal the steps of that plan to us.

The basis for that assurance lies in the nature of God. For it is God's nature to reveal Himself and His purposes to man. When I was in seminary I learned the famous definition of God contained in the Westminster Shorter Catechism: "God is a Spirit, infinite, eternal, and unchangeable, in His being, wisdom, power, holiness, justice, goodness, and truth." The first time a person hears that definition, I suppose he inevitably thinks that just about everything that could possibly be said about God is wrapped up in it, for the definition is long. And yet, as I began to memorize and study it, I learned that it was far from comprehensive. For one thing, there is no mention of God's being love. God is certainly infinite, eternal, and unchangeable in His love. Moreover, today I believe I should also like to see God's desire to reveal Himself to man included. I should like to say, "God is a Spirit, infinite, eternal, and unchangeable, in His being, wisdom, power, holiness, justice, goodness, truth, love, and desire to reveal Himself to man."

In one sense all that God has ever done has been directed toward that end. When God made the world, it was to reveal Himself to those who would eventually live on it. Creation reveals God. Hence, Paul said, "For since the creation of the world His invisible attributes, His eternal power and divine nature, have been clearly seen, being understood through what has been made, so that they are without excuse" (Romans 1:20). When God caused the Scriptures of the Old and New Testaments to be written, that too was to reveal Himself to man. Finally, just as God revealed His power in nature and His purposes in Scripture, so did He reveal His personality in His Son, the Lord Jesus Christ. That is why Jesus could say, "He who has seen Me has seen the Father" (John 14:9).

In addition, God's revelation always involves a disclosure of His will for the individual person. On that basis Donald Grey Barnhouse used to say that it was actually impossible for a Christian who wanted to know the will of God for his life not to know it. That statement by Barnhouse brings us to the first of the great biblical principles by which a Christian may unquestionably come to know God's will. For the Bible teaches that, if you really want to know God's will, you must be willing to do it even before you know what it is. That is clearly taught in John 7:17: "If any man is willing do His will [the phrase means "wants or determines to do it"], he shall know of the teaching, whether it is of God, or whether I speak from Myself." Although Jesus was literally speaking of the rejection of His doctrine by the Jewish leaders, He was actually teaching the great principle that knowing the will of God consists largely in being willing to do it.

If we are to come to the point where we are willing in advance to do God's will, we must recognize first that in ourselves we do not want to do it. If we say to ourselves, "Oh, but I have always wanted to do the Lord's will," we are kidding ourselves. For "the mind set on the flesh is hostile toward God; for it does not subject itself to the law of God, for it is not even able to do so" (Romans 8:7). There is a great deal of the fleshly, or carnal, mind in all of us.

We are all somewhat like the Israelites when they first came out of Egypt. They were a huge company. The Bible says that there were 600,000 men, and in addition to that were the women and children. So the total must have been in the neighborhood of two million people. That great host was traveling through the desert, where the temperature goes much above one hundred degrees in the daytime and often falls to below freezing at night. In those extremes of hot and cold, the people would have perished if God had not performed a great miracle to save them.

The miracle was the miracle of the cloud, which signified God's presence with the people and led them in their desert wanderings. The cloud was large enough to spread out over the camp of the Israelites. It provided shade during the daytime; and it gave warmth by night, when it turned into a pillar of fire. It was also the banner by which they regulated their march. When the cloud moved, the people moved, and when the cloud stopped, they stopped. One of our great hymns describes it by saying,

> Round each habitation hovering,
>   See the cloud and fire appear,
> For a glory and a covering,
>   Showing that the Lord is near.
> Thus deriving from their banner,
>   Light by night, and shade by day,
> Safe they feed upon the manna
>   Which he gives them when they pray.

The cloud was the single most distinguishing feature of their encampment.

Now we must imagine how it would have been when the cloud moved forward and how weary the people would have become of following it. We read in the final verses of Exodus, "Whenever the cloud was taken up from over the tabernacle, the sons of Israel would set out; but if the cloud was not taken up, then they did not set out until the day when it was taken up" (Exodus 40:36-37). Sometimes it moved often; at other times it did not move at all. We must imagine a family coming to a stop under the cloud's guidance in the middle of a hot afternoon and immediately beginning to unpack their baggage. They take down their bedding and set up their tent. No sooner has it all been arranged, however, than someone cries out, "The cloud is moving." So they repack their baggage and start to go on again. One hour later the cloud stops. They say, "We'll just leave our things packed this time and sleep on the ground." Well, they do. But the cloud stays that night and all the next day and all that week. As they are going into the second week, the mother says, "Well, we might as well get it over with." So they unpack. And immediately the cloud begins to move forward again.

The people must have hated the moving of the cloud by which God guided them. But no matter how much they hated the cloud, they still had to follow its guidance. If someone had said, "I don't care if the cloud is moving; I'm going to stay right here," the cloud would have gone on; and that person would have died in the heat of the desert, or he would have frozen at night. The people hated God's leading. But by that means God was molding a nation of rabble, of slaves, into a disciplined force that would one day be able to conquer the land of Canaan. He was teaching them absolute obedience.

It is the same with us. Neither you nor I naturally want God's will; we want our own will. We will always hate God's way—and particularly His way of training us to be soldiers. Nevertheless, we must go through with it. For through that training we learn to say, "Father, even though I do not naturally want your will, nevertheless, I know that it is the best thing for me; and it is necessary for my spiritual training. Lead me in the way I should go." And God will do that. To know God's will we must first come to the point where we want to do it.

The second great principle for knowing the will of God is that nothing can be the will of God that is contrary to the Word of God. The God who is leading you now is the God who inspired the Bible, and He is not contradictory in His commandments. Consequently, nothing can be the will of God for you that is not in accordance with His Word.

In the Bible, God's will is expressed in great principles. Take John 6:39-40, for instance. I call this verse the will of God for all unbelievers. It says, "And this is the will of Him who sent Me, that . . . every one who beholds the Son, and believes in Him, may have eternal life; and I Myself will raise him up on the last day." If you are not a Christian, God generally is not at all interested in telling you whether you should accept a job with General Motors or Dupont or whether you should enlist in the army. He is not interested in showing you whom you should marry. He is interested in whether or not you will believe in Jesus Christ and receive Him as your personal Savior. God's will for you starts there. That is His will. You must accept that demand before you can begin to go forward on any other level.

Another passage that expresses one of those great principles is Romans 12:1-2. It is an expression of God's will for the Christian. "I urge you therefore, brethren, by the mercies of God, to present your bodies a living and holy sacrifice, acceptable to God, which is your spiritual service of worship. And do not be conformed to this world, but be transformed by the renewing of your mind, that you may prove what the will of God is, that which is good and acceptable and perfect." If you are a Christian, you can take it as an unchangeable principle that anything that contributes to your growth in holiness is an aspect of God's will for you. And anything that hinders your growth in holiness is not His will. God is interested in having you become like His Son, the Lord Jesus.

Colossians 3:23 is an expression of God's will for your work. It says, "Whatever you do, do your work heartily, as for the Lord rather than for men." That is especially applicable to young people. A member of my congregation once remarked that all too often young people interpret a difficulty in their work or schooling as being an indication that what they are doing is not God's will for them, when actually it is probably God's indication that they should work harder at it. This verse tells us that God wants us to do well everything we are given to do.

A principle that is closely related to that one is found in Ephesians 6:5-6: "Slaves, be obedient to those who are your masters according to the flesh, with fear and trembling, in the sincerity of your heart, as to Christ; not by way of eyeservice, as menpleasers, but as slaves of Christ, doing the will of God from the heart." This principle is for you if you have a difficult boss or a difficult teacher. The Bible says it is God's will that you should avoid gossiping about him and, instead, work as well as you are able under his guidance. And you should do it not only when he is watching but when he is not watching—as unto the Lord and not unto men.

Perhaps you are saying, "Well, those principles are good, but they do not touch the small things with which I am wrestling." You want to know whether as a Christian you should go to the movies, join a bridge club, make friends with the people at work, join in social drinking, or some other thing. Let me give you a final principle that covers most of those. "Finally, brethren, whatever is true, whatever is honorable, whatever is right, whatever is pure, whatever is lovely, whatever is of good repute, if there is any excellence and if anything worthy of praise, let your mind dwell on these things" (Philippians 4:8). God says that you are to pursue the best things in life. If the things you are questioning are the best things for you—and some of them can be—then do them. If not, you are to go another way. Just be sure that you take your guidelines from Scripture.

The third principle is also important. It is the principle of daily and even hourly fellowship with the Lord. Psalm 32:8 states it like this: "I will instruct you and teach you in the way which you should go; I will counsel you with My eye upon you." Clearly, if God is to guide us, He must first catch our eyes. And that means that we must look to Him regularly throughout the day.

Let me illustrate with a story. I have a good friend who is a gospel singer and who, for many years, was a bachelor. He once said, "You know, Jim, it is always easy to find a Christian girl to marry. And it is always easy to find a beautiful girl to marry. But it is not so easy to find a beautiful Christian girl to marry." I suppose he was partly right. At any rate, he eventually found the girl and married her. She was perfect in every way but one. At times she talked with a very shrill voice, especially in the presence of company. And because he was a baritone, her voice often grated on his ears. That was the making of a serious problem in their marriage.

The Lord had given that man a great deal of tact, among other talents, and he used his tact to go about solving the problem in this way: one day he came to his wife and said to her, "Dear, do you know the first thing that a drama coach teaches an actress when she begins training?"

His wife said no.

"He teaches her to lower her voice. By nature, a woman's voice is shrill, but it becomes warm and pleasing when it is lowered about an octave. A drama coach will teach an actress to say a phrase, count down seven notes, repeat it again, and then practice that repeatedly. I think your voice would be improved if you would do that."

When my friend's wife agreed, they arranged a signal by which she would be reminded to lower her voice in the presence of company. The signal was for him to tuck in his chin.

My friend told me that there were times when that produced the funniest effect you could imagine. There they would be, sitting around the dining room table talking, and his wife's voice would be rising higher and higher. He would tuck in his chin and look at her. Then, often right in the middle of one of her sentences, she would catch his eye. She would notice his chin, and her voice would drop like a lead marshmallow and go on at a pitch one octave lower. She saw the sign when she looked at her husband.

It must be the same in our daily walk with the Lord. The Lord knows that we will go astray. It is out nature to go astray. Our speech or conduct will become displeasing. We will always do things that displease Him. But we must get into the habit of looking to Him often—in church, during our quiet time, at various periods in our day—to catch His eye. For, if we do, we will find Him watching. He will direct us. And He will guide us with His eye upon us.

There is only one more point that I need to make, and it is not difficult at all. If you are serious about knowing the Lord's will and honestly seek it, then you must be prepared for the Lord to guide you into new ways. If there is one thing that I have most learned about the Lord's guidance, it is that He does not often lead us in old ways. God is creative. He is infinite. So, naturally, He is infinite in His plans for His children.

David Wilkerson, who has been greatly blessed in a unique ministry to teenagers in New York City, told in the opening chapter of his book *The Cross and the Switchblade* how he was led into new paths in his ministry. He had been a Pentecostal preacher in central Pennsylvania. By his personal standards he was doing quite well. The church had grown. There were several new buildings. Yet he was discontented. One day he decided to spend the late evening hours, when he had been used to watching television, praying. He sold the television set after much hesitation and began to spend time with the Lord. He did that for some time. Eventually, out of those times he was led to begin his work helping young people in Manhattan who were caught up in drug addiction and delinquency. God's will for David Wilkerson led a country preacher into the heart and the heartbreak of the city.

It will also be true for you. If you seek God's will, determining to do it even before you know what it is, if you look to Him while responding to His voice in the Bible, then God will reveal His way and direct you in ever widening and ever more interesting paths. He will be close to you, and He *will* lead you in the way that you should go.

5

How to Know God's Will in Doubtful Situations

Should you as a Christian drink alcohol or not? Will it be harmful to your testimony if you play cards? Can you enter politics? Can you work for a company that manufactures war materials? To what extent can a believer adopt the standards of his time and society? Questions such as those are asked by Christians at many different points in their lives; and they are important, for they concern the problems of regulating conduct in areas of life where the Bible is not entirely explicit. How do you deal with them?

You need to recognize first that although many of the things that trouble Christians are silly and do not deserve much attention, not all of them are. Consequently you must not make the mistake of avoiding all serious thought about them.

For instance, in this country there are often many don'ts in Christian circles that I am convinced have in themselves little or nothing to do with Christianity. "Should I permit my son to wear his hair long?" is one of them. "How much should we use contemporary music in our church?" is another. In some circles those behavioral patterns are almost a badge of a person's or church's commitment to Jesus Christ. And yet, in other circles, among believers who are entirely conservative and firmly committed to the Lord, those things mean nothing at all. Instead, they may believe the touchstone of real commitment lies in observing Sunday as a day of rest, free from normal activities. In Switzerland women are noted for their piety if they wear long hair; if it is short, in line with modern fashions, many will think them to be backsliding in their Christianity.

Some doubtful things are unimportant, but other doubtful items deserve more serious attention. Elizabeth Elliot, the widow of Jim Elliot, who was killed by the Auca Indians in Ecuador, has written about one of those problems in a little book called *The Liberty of Obedience.*

She had always had the idea, perhaps as the product of her Christian upbringing, that there was a certain type of clothing that was right for a Christian to wear. And, conversely, there was clothing that was wrong. But then she went to Ecuador, and she found herself in the midst of a tropical people who wore little or no clothing at all. What did her standards have to do with them? Should she dress new converts? Should their standards prevail? She said that the problem became even more complex when she realized in time that, although the women in the tribe wore almost no clothing, they were nevertheless conscious of the proper and modest ways to walk, sit, and stand. The entire problem forced her to ask herself if there was anything inherently Christian or non-Christian in the way we dress in America.

Another problem with an uncertain answer is alcohol. Should a Christian drink? Does the level of society in which a Christian finds himself matter? I tend to think that something as obviously harmful as alcohol has been in many instances should automatically be avoided; and I admire men, such as the chairman of the board of a large US corporation, who do not drink.

But what happens to that conviction when you go to France—as I did as a young boy—and see the leading deacon of an evangelical Protestant church going around a large ring of children at a Sunday school picnic pouring wine? I know that part of the reason he did it was to prevent their getting sick on the water in a rural area, but the main point was his attitude toward alcohol. That was obviously quite different in France, even among people who believed all that the most conservative Christians in America believe about the gospel.

Comparisons such as those defeat any approach to the problem through rules and regulations. And any such comparison turns us back once more to the principles of Scripture. I should like to suggest three great principles that will help any Christian in at least 99 percent of his difficulties. Those principles are found throughout Scripture, but they are summarized in three important verses: Romans 6:14, 1 Corinthians 6:12 (also 10:23), and Philippians 4:8. Those verses tell you that you are to live (as you have been saved) by grace; that you are to think first, last, and always of others; and that you are to pursue the highest things.

The first principle is that you are under grace, not under law. "For sin shall not be master over you, for you are not under law, but under grace" (Romans 6:14). Whatever the answer may be to the problems of doubtful things, it will not come as a result of regulations. The answer will never be found by organizing a body of Christians to declare whether or not music, hair length, alcohol, cards, the Masons, war, or whatever it may be, are proper.

Historically, the problem was fought to a decisive conclusion in the first generation of the church. Because of the wide dispersion of Jews throughout the Roman world in the centuries before Christ, there was hardly a congregation of believers during the first century that did not consist of a mixture of Jews and Gentiles, even in the most Gentile cities of the empire. Somehow, probably because of their own religious and social training, the Jewish Christians got the idea that the Gentile believers should submit to the ceremonial laws of Israel, and the result was a tremendous battle. At one point the apostle Paul fought almost single-handedly against that idea. For a time, even Peter was carried away with the error, but Paul resisted him (Galatians 2:11-14). Once Paul defended the case for Gentile (and Jewish) liberty before the other apostles in Jerusalem. On that occasion Peter sided with Paul and said, "Now therefore why do you put God to the test by placing upon the neck of the disciples a yoke which neither our fathers nor we have been able to bear? But we believe that we are saved through the grace of the Lord Jesus, in the same way as they" (Acts 15:10-11). In the early church the battle against legalism was won for pure grace.

It is also true, however, that the same verse that speaks against a solution by means of rules speaks against yet another error that is also a wrong approach to the problem. That is the error of license, the teaching that, because you are no longer under law but under grace, you can go on doing as you please. That is, "Let us sin that grace may abound." That error pretends to be logical, but it is not. It is infernal. And Paul did not hesitate to say so. "What then? Shall we sin because we are not under law but under grace? May it never be!" (Romans 6:15). He added, "But now having been freed from sin and enslaved to God, you derive your benefit, resulting in sanctification, and the outcome, eternal life" (v. 22).

Paul's argument was that life by grace actually leads to holiness, and therefore you should not fear to abolish rules as an answer to the problems of Christian conduct.

The way that works may be illustrated by comparing two types of marriage. One type of marriage is founded on law. In that marriage the wife says something like this: "I know that you are going off to that office party tonight, and I know that dozens of those young secretaries will be there. Don't you dare look at any of them! Because if you do, and I hear about it, I'll really lay into you when you get home. And be back by ten-thirty." Well, if the wife says that, the husband is likely to go off saying to himself, "So that's what she wants, is it? Well, I'll just stay out as long as I please and do as I please." There will be no end of friction, for legalism does not promote happiness or fidelity in marriage.

The other type of marriage is one in which there is love rather than law. Each partner knows the faults of the other, but they both know that they love each other anyway and have forgiven those faults in advance. Are they happy? Certainly they are happy. And they are faithful in the relationship. In a similar way, the grace of God never makes rebels; it makes men and women who love God and desire to please Him.

The second principle for determining God's will in doubtful matters is that, although all things are permissible for the Christian because he is not under law but under grace, still all things are not helpful and should therefore be avoided. That is true for two reasons: first, because the thing itself may gain a harmful control over him and, second, because through him it may hurt other Christians.

The first reason is given in 1 Corinthians 6:12: "All things are lawful for me, but not all things are profitable. All things are lawful for me, but I will not be mastered by anything." Paul knew that God had not set him free from sin and the law in order for him to become captive to mere things.

The guiding principle here is whether you, as a Christian, are using things or things are using you. Take food for example. Nothing can be as obviously good for a person as food; it is necessary for bodily strength as well as mental health. But it is possible for a person to become so addicted to overeating that the good end is thwarted and the person's health endangered. Hence, certain eating habits should be avoided (v. 13). The second of Paul's examples is sex (vv. 13-20). That too is good. It is a gift of God. Within the bonds of marriage it is a force for strength in the home, as well as being an expression of close union. But it, too, can be destructive. It can control the person instead of the person controlling it. In that form sex can destroy the very values it was created to maintain. The Bible teaches that the Christian must never use things—food, sex, drugs, alcohol, cars, homes, stocks, or whatever—in such a way that he actually falls under their power. In some of those cases, such as in the case of habit-forming drugs, I would think that 1 Corinthians 6:12 is an unequivocable warning to avoid them.

Later on in 1 Corinthians Paul gives another reason why all things are not helpful: the freedom of one believer may hurt the spiritual growth of another. Paul said, "All things are lawful, but not all things are profitable. All things are lawful, but not all things edify" (1 Corinthians 10:23). The verses that follow show that he is thinking of the well-being and growth of fellow Christians.

I do not believe that verse means you have to take your standard of conduct entirely from what other Christians say or think. If you do that, you will either become hypocritical or go mad. Ethel Barrett, who is well known for her Bible story work among children, has told of her early experiences with matters of dress when she first began to travel about the country. Originally she came from California, and her standards of dress were formed by the climate and style of California. Hence, her clothes were bright, and she wore a good deal of makeup and large hats. When she went to the East and began to work there, she soon met some to whom her standards of dress seemed unspiritual. They said, "Why is she dressing like that? That is no way for a Christian to dress." Well, she was young in those days, and she took it to heart. She changed her clothes; she stopped wearing makeup. It was not long, however, before some remarks got back to her: "Why does she have to look so drab and unpleasant? She would have a much more effective and spiritual ministry if she would brighten herself up a bit." Ethel Barrett learned through the experience that you cannot take all your standards of conduct from other Christians, and she was right. The verse does not mean that you are to allow the prejudices and viewpoints of others to dictate your pattern of behavior.

Still, the verse does mean something. For it says that there are situations in which we must avoid certain things, even if they are right in themselves, lest they be detrimental to others. Let me give you an example. Suppose you have been witnessing to a young man who has been having a hard time overcoming a disposition to sexual sins. He has become a Christian, but the lure of the flesh is still with him. Well, this verse means that you had better not encourage him to see television shows or read books that may cause him to dwell on sensual things. What is more, you had better not watch or read them yourself, for he may be harmed by your freedom. In the same way, you are not to serve fattening foods to a Christian for whom weight control is a serious problem; and for his sake, if necessary, you are to avoid them also.

Moreover, you are to be consistent in your abstinence, for you must not appear double-faced or hypocritical. And you must sometimes be consistent over a long period of time. Paul wrote, "Therefore, if food causes my brother to stumble, I will never eat meat again, that I might not cause my brother to stumble" (1 Corinthians 8:13). Just think: never again! This from the same apostle who defended the cause of Christian liberty successfully before the Jerusalem apostles! You must remember that it will be costly if you are to be careful of the effect of your conduct upon others.

I think the final principle best helps direct our conduct in doubtful areas: "Finally, brethren, whatever is true, whatever is honorable, whatever is right, whatever is pure, whatever is lovely, whatever is of good repute, if there is any excellence and if anything worthy of praise, let your mind dwell on these things" (Philippians 4:8). According to that verse, the Christian is to decide between doubtful things by choosing the best.

That does not exclude the best things in our society, whether explicitly Christian or not, for the meat of the verse lies in the fact (not always noticed by commentators and Bible teachers) that the virtues mentioned here are pagan virtues. Those words do not occur in the great lists of Christian virtues, lists that include love, joy, peace, longsuffering, and so forth. On the whole they are taken from Greek ethics and from the writings of Greek philosophers. Hence, in using those words, Paul was actually sanctifying, as it were, the generally accepted virtues of pagan morality. He is saying that, although the pursuit of the best things by Christians will necessarily mean the pursuit of fellowship with God, pursuit of the will of God, pursuit of all means to advance the claims of the gospel, and the pursuit of other spiritual things also, it will not mean the exclusion of the best values that the world has to offer. The things that are acknowledged to be honorable by the best men everywhere are also worthy to be cultivated by Christians. Consequently, as a Christian, you can love all that is true, honest, right, pure, lovely, and of good repute, wherever you find it. You can rejoice in the best of art and literature. You can thrill to great music. You can thrive on beautiful architecture. You can also thank God for giving men the ability, even in their fallen state, to create such beauty.

Moreover, as you use this principle for determining God's will in doubtful things, you can also take confidence from the promise of God's presence that accompanies it. Paul often wrote parenthetically in his letters, and he did so here also. The result is that the first half of verse 9 partially distorts the meaning of the sentence. Verse 9 reads, "The things you have learned and received and heard and seen in me, practice these things; and the God of peace shall be with you." You would tend to think that the promise of God's presence is attached to the first half of the verse. Actually, it is attached to verse 8, and the promise is: "Whatever is true, honest, right, pure, lovely, and of good repute, dwell on these things . . . and the God of peace shall be with you."

When you pursue the highest things in life, both spiritually and secularly, then the God of peace will be with you. And you will have the confidence that He will bless and guide you as you seek to please Him.

6

How to Get Along With Other Christians

Have you ever had trouble getting along with another Christian? Perhaps you found it difficult because the other person was unwilling to respond to you or because of what you suspected was a failure in yourself. Many Christians have the same problem. In fact, even in the New Testament church at Philippi, two good friends of the apostle Paul were having similar problems. Paul gave them some good advice, and I am sure that his advice will be helpful to you, too.

Apparently there had been trouble at Philippi. It was not terrible trouble, but it was serious enough to have worried Paul. Two of the women—Euodia and Syntyche—were at odds with one another, and the disagreement had grown to the point where it could hinder the unity and effectiveness of the church. Paul wished to warn his friends of this danger and to avoid the problems that might come. So he wrote to them, asking them to forget their differences, work for the same goal, and be happy together as Christians.

He wrote, "I urge Euodia and I urge Syntyche to live in harmony in the Lord. Indeed, true comrade, I ask you also to help these women who have shared my struggle in the cause of the gospel, together with Clement also, and the rest of my fellow workers, whose names are in the book of life. Rejoice in the Lord always; again I will say, rejoice! Let your forbearing spirit be known to all men. The Lord is near" (Philippians 4:2-5).

First, Paul said that Euodia and Syntyche were to "live in harmony of the Lord." That means that we are to have the mind of Christ, and, since Christ was not proud or defensive of His own interests, we are not to be proud or defensive either.

Paul had the same thing in mind when he wrote earlier, "Have this attitude in yourselves which was also in Christ Jesus" (Philippians 2:5). He was not speaking of the doctrines that Christ taught, although they are important. He was speaking of the attitude that Jesus had in relation to others. It was the mind of one who did not consider equality with God something to be retained at all costs but who came to earth in order to die for the salvation and well-being of others.

In other words, to be humble you need to stop thinking about yourself all the time. You need to stop comparing yourself with your boss, the secretary who sits next to you, the other Sunday school teacher, or whoever it is who rubs you the wrong way. Instead you need to think of what you can do to help that person.

That humility will never occur apart from a personal and intimate walk with God, for in ourselves we do not like humility. And we cannot achieve it without Him. If you are far from the Lord, then frictions will inevitably spring up between you and other Christians. The things they say will irk you. The things they do will get under your skin and fester. If you do not want that to happen, then you must maintain a close and personal fellowship with the Lord.

You see, Paul wanted his admonition to the women at Philippi to come down to the personal level. For he knew, as we all should know, that the effectiveness of the Christian warfare depends upon the conduct of the individual Christian soldier. As the church impinges upon the world, it is a little like a triangle. It has a broad base composed of many believers and many doctrines. But the impact point is the apex, and the apex is the individual Christian. The individual is what the world sees. The individual is the one who either promotes or hinders harmony. And who is the individual? You! And I! If there is to be Christian unity, you and I must maintain our walk with the Lord.

Second, Paul said that Christian unity is something we must work at. He called attention to that step toward unity by referring to his fellow workers at Philippi and to the one who was a "true comrade" in that ministry. It is not enough, he implied, for Christians merely to think about unity. They must work for it, and they must work together.

Another way of saying the same thing is that reading this chapter will not be enough. Positive thinking is not enough. If you are to get along with another Christian with whom you have difficulty, you must roll up your sleeves and work together with him. The problem that he is facing is a good place to start, whatever it may be. Clean his garage with him. Help her with her shopping. Then, when you run out of those things, go visit a person who is sick, teach a class, start a home Bible study. *But do it together.*

Paul was looking back to the glorious days that he had spent in Philippi among the Christians. He was thinking of the great joy he had known as he had worked with them for spiritual ends. Now that unity was being threatened. So he said to them, "Keep on. Do not let your unity be ruined by friction between your members. Work together. Make sure your unity can be seen in your actions."

The third step in getting along with other Christians is to rejoice in the Lord. Paul said this in Philippians 4:4: "Rejoice in the Lord always; again I will say, rejoice!" Paul knew that if a Christian is rejoicing in God's mercy and goodness to him, he is not so likely to be nit-picking with his fellow Christians. If your thoughts are filled with God, you will not be seeing another's bad temper, laziness, or unreliability.

The word *rejoice* is interesting, for it is only a variant form of the word *joy,* which is one of the great Christian virtues, the fruit of God's Spirit. (We will look at it in greater detail in chapter 12.) Joy is supernatural; it does not depend on circumstances. We have all seen the Charlie Brown cartoon that defines happiness as a warm puppy. But suppose there is no puppy. Well, then there is no happiness. Happiness depends on the things we have or can acquire. For some it is money. For others it is fame. For some it is power or good looks. But it is all external. When those things go, happiness goes with them. It is not that way with joy. Joy issues from the nature of God, and it is intended to well up within those in whom God's Spirit dwells.

Things may happen to the Christian that no one, including the Christian, would be happy about. But there can still be joy. The Christian who is filled with supernatural, abounding joy will not be finding grounds for disagreement with his fellow Christians.

The fourth step is given in verse 5. There Paul said that Christians should let their forbearing spirit [moderation, KJV]* be known to all men." Moderation here is not the same thing as temperance, which is mentioned as a fruit of the Spirit in Galatians 5. It is a different word from that. In fact, it is an unusual Greek word, one that does not occur in the classical Greek before Paul's time. He may have coined it. Literally, it means "reasonableness" or "being reasonable." It conveys a warning not to be unduly rigorous about unimportant matters.

That does not mean that Christians are to be compromising in their doctrinal beliefs. Paul was not talking about doctrine here any more than he was talking about doctrine when he referred to the attitude of Christ in verse 2. He was not talking about compromising with the world's standards of conduct, either. He had already written that Christians should live as "blameless and innocent, children of God above reproach in the midst of a crooked and perverse generation, among whom you appear as lights in the world" (Philippians 2:15). And he wrote to the Roman Christians that they were not to be "conformed to this

---

*King James Version.

world" but "transformed by the renewing of your mind" (Romans 12:2).

Actually, what Paul was saying is that those who profess the name of Christ should be a bit bending in their conduct, especially where other Christians are concerned. They should not be brittle. We are not to have a personality so inflexible that people bounce off it like a tennis ball bouncing off a stone wall. We are to listen to people, even to tolerate their errors for a time (if you will), in order that God in His time might use us better to encourage them in their walk with the Lord.

This should be especially applicable in Christian families. Often children rebel against the gospel and against their parents; and they do so many times, I am convinced, simply because the parents have been too rigid and too doctrinaire in their training. Here, too, there must be moderation; and it must be an aspect of that yieldingness with one another to which Christians are called.

None of those high standards of conduct is easy—to be humble, to work with someone who is difficult, to be filled with joy, to be reasonable. And, let us admit it; the difficulty of living them is where the problem of unity lies. It is one thing to say to each other, "Well, let us be of the same mind and work together. Let us rejoice. Let us show moderation." But it is quite another thing to put the words into practice. Fortunately, Paul also knew the difficulty. As a result, he gave us the solution even to this problem.

Have you ever noticed how many times he spoke of being "in the Lord Jesus Christ" in the first four verses of this chapter? Three times! And once he reminded them that "the Lord is near." The solution is the Lord Jesus Christ. It is He who will do in the lives of yielded Christians what they might judge impossible.

You can learn to get along with other Christians only as you surrender yourself to Christ and seek His will, as His Holy Spirit enters your life and begins to make you into the man or woman that He would have you be.

7

How to Have a Happy Marriage

Marriage can be one of the most beautiful relationships on earth. But it can also be one of the most miserable. What makes the difference? What makes just any old marriage a happy marriage?

It is easy to say that in order to be happy a marriage should be based on Christian principles. But then we must go on to ask, "What makes a marriage Christian? What does a Christian marriage involve? What are God's purposes in marriage?"

Those questions can only begin to be answered when we recognize that God is the author of marriage and that He has established it as the most important illustration in all of life of how He joins true believers to the Lord Jesus Christ in faith forever. The basis of everything to be said about Christian marriage lies in the fact that marriage is a divine institution.

I suppose that I perform between half a dozen and a dozen weddings each year; and at each of them I begin by calling attention to the truth that God has instituted marriage, for this truth is of prime importance in the marriage service. I say, "Dearly beloved, we are assembled here in the presence of God, to join this man and this woman in holy marriage; which is instituted by God, regulated by His commandments, blessed by our Lord Jesus Christ, and to be held in honor among all men. Let us therefore reverently remember that God has established and sanctified marriage for the welfare and happiness of mankind." In the prayer that follows I give thanks to God for the state of marriage and ask His blessing on the ensuing service.

God has established marriage. That is the point. It follows from this that marriage must be governed and directed by His rules, especially if it is to result in the happiness and joy that all men acknowledge should belong to it.

Who originally made the race male and female? God did (Genesis 1:27). Who commanded, "Be fruitful and multiply" (Genesis 1:28)? God. Who said, "It is not good for the man to be alone; I will make him an help fit for him" (Genesis 2:18)? God. It was God who brought the first bride to the first bridegroom and thus established the first human family (Genesis 2:22). God's word declares, "For this cause a man shall leave his father and his mother, and shall cleave to his wife; and they shall become one flesh" (Genesis 2:24). In His teaching on divorce, Jesus reinforced the teaching that marriage is a divine institution (Matthew 19:4-9). It is for this reason that the Church speaks for "holy matrimony." For although we do not believe, as some do, that marriage is a sacrament of the church, we do believe that God has established it, that His laws should regulate it, and that it is far from being a merely civil or social arrangement.

A practical consequence follows upon that. For if it is true that God has established the state of marriage, then we must never make fun of it or of anything connected with the marriage relationship. Donald Grey Barnhouse used to say, "Bite your tongue before you will ever say, 'Well, I want you to meet the old ball and chain' or 'Here's the jailer.'" Walter A. Maier, who produced the most valuable book on marriage that I have read, has written, "To speak disdainfully of married life, to invoke upon it sophisticated sarcasm, is to exalt the puny errors of pigmy minds over the eternal truth of heaven—to blaspheme God."[1] Both of them are right. Consequently, neither you nor I should joke about marriage.

Moreover, the fact that God has established marriage means that you and I are to get our ideas about it, not from the books we may read or from the movies, but from God Himself and from the Bible. I suppose that over the years I have read perhaps forty books about marriage and sexual problems, and the general impression I have had from the non-Christian books (and sometimes the Christian ones) is that marriage is primarily a matter of sexual compatibility and adjustment. That is part of the truth, of course. But at best it is one-sided, and by itself it is only slightly less misleading than the marriages in movies, where marriage is either a farce or else the institutionalization of romantic love. Neither of those is right.

What the Bible teaches about marriage is quite different. For instance, as far back as in the early pages of Genesis we read that a man shall "leave his father and his mother, and shall cleave to his wife; and they shall become one flesh" (Genesis 2:24). We must not make the mistake of thinking that that refers only to a sexual union, for the Bible uses the word *flesh* in a far broader sense than the meanings we give to it. The word means the person as a whole. Thus, the union, in a certain sense, makes one person of those who were two persons before. C. S. Lewis has argued that marriage results in something like a two-part mechanism, like a lock and key or a violin and its bow. I would much rather call it a single organism, in which the relationship of a wife to a husband or husband to wife is like that of a person's hand to his head or his heart to his mind.

Another way of saying the same thing is to point out that man is a trinity as God is a Trinity. He has a body, a soul, and a spirit. The union of one man with one woman in marriage must be a union on each of those three levels if marriage is to be what God intended it to be and the union is to be lasting.

There must be a union of body with body, first of all, which is to say there must be a valid sexual relationship. That is important. For that reason all the branches of the Christian church acknowledge that a marriage has not actually taken place until it has been consummated. If sexual union does not take place or cannot take place, then the marriage can be annulled as invalid. I always tell couples that that is a vital aspect of the marriage relationship. According to the Bible, neither the man nor the woman is to defraud the other of the sexual experience. The quickest way for the marriage to end up in trouble is for the wife to have a headache every night and go to sleep early to avoid sex, or for the husband to lose interest in his wife romantically and to spend his nights elsewhere or with the boys. Sex must be a regular expression of the relationship.

On the other hand, if the relationship is based upon nothing but sex—in other words, if it is a marriage of body with body alone and not of soul with soul and spirit with spirit—then the marriage is weak and inadequate and is headed for the divorce courts. When the glamour of physical attraction wears off, as it always does if there is nothing more to sustain it, the relationship is finished. There is either total indifference, a divorce, or adultery.

A better marriage than that is a marriage that is also a union of soul with soul. The word *soul* had almost passed out of use in the English language until the blacks of our day revived it. It is a good word, and we would have been poorer for its loss. It refers to the intellectual and emotional side of a person's nature, involving all the characteristics that we associate with the functioning of the mind. Hence, a marriage that involves a union of souls is a marriage in which a couple shares an interest in the same things—the same books, the same shows, the same friends—and seeks to establish a meeting of the minds (as it were) both intellectually and emotionally. Such marriages will always last longer.

I believe that at this point a special word must be said to Christians who are married. For whenever a minister speaks like this to Christians, many race ahead of him to point three and conclude that, because their marriages are unions of a spirit with spirit, they do not need to worry about a union of their minds or souls. That is not right. Not only do we need to worry about it at times, we also need to work toward it. A husband and wife should share books and other interests. An emotional and intellectual union does not in itself come naturally.

What does a girl have in her mind when she marries a young man? What is her vision of this new husband? Well, it has something to do with her father and whether she liked him or rebelled against him. It has a little bit of Cary Grant mixed up in it, and perhaps a little of James Bond or Johnny Carson or her minister. What is the vision of the husband? Keith Miller, the author of the best-selling book *A Taste of New Wine,* said that his vision was probably a combination of St. Theresa, Elizabeth Taylor and Betty Crocker. Every man puts his own set of names into those categories.

Now, what happens when a girl with a vision of Cary Grant and a man with a vision of Elizabeth Taylor get married and begin to find out that the other person is not much like their vision? One of two things! Either they center their minds on the difference between the ideal and what they are increasingly finding the other person to be like and then try, either openly or subversively, to push the other person into that image. Or, by the grace of God, they increasingly come to accept the other person as he is, including his standards of how they themselves should be, and then under God seek to conform to the best and most uplifting of those standards.

It must be one or the other of those ways. Keith Miller has written, "The soul of a marriage can be a trysting place where two people can come together quietly from the struggles of the world and feel safe, accepted, and loved . . . or it can be a battleground where two egos are locked in a lifelong struggle for supremacy, a battle which is for the most part invisible to the rest of the world."[2] If you and I are to have the former in our marriages, then we must work toward it. And we must do it by cultivating the interests and the aspirations of the other party.

A true marriage must be a marriage of body with body and

soul with soul. But it must also be a marriage of spirit with spirit. It is for that reason that the only marriages that can approximate the kind of marriage God intended to exist in this world are Christian marriages. What does that mean—a marriage of spirit with spirit? Primarily it means that both the husband and the wife must be Christians, for the unsaved person possesses a spirit only in the sense that he supports a vacuum at the center of his life that can only be filled by God. He has a spirit, but the spirit has died—just as Adam's spirit died when he disobeyed God and ran from Him. The only persons who possess a live spirit are those who have been touched by the Holy Spirit and have entered into God's family by faith in the Lord Jesus Christ. Hence, only those can be married in the full sense of the word—body with body, soul with soul, and spirit with spirit.

If you are a Christian, you must marry another Christian, or else you must not marry at all. If you do marry a non-Christian, then you are willfully choosing much unhappiness, for you will be unable to share that which is most real and most precious to you.

What will happen to you can be illustrated from the case of Solomon. Solomon was the recipient of many blessings from God, first, because of God's promises to his father David, and then because of the fact that Solomon had himself determined to walk in the Lord's way. However, after the Temple was finished and Solomon was at ease in Jerusalem, he began to get ideas, one of which was to marry the daughter of the Pharaoh of Egypt. That was not God's will for him, for the princess of Egypt did not worship Jehovah. It was one step in Solomon's downfall. Nevertheless, he did it even though he knew it was wrong, as one verse in the story tells us. We read in 2 Chronicles 8:11: "Then Solomon brought Pharaoh's daughter up from the city of David to the house which he had built for her; for he said, 'My wife shall not dwell in the house of David king of Israel, because the places are holy where the ark of the LORD has entered.'" In other words Solomon was saying, "I recognize that this woman does not fit in with the things that I know to be true about God;

and whenever I bring her around the palace of David or the Temple, I feel guilty, and my conscience bothers me. The only solution is to build her another house and hereafter to live my life in as nearly separate but equal compartments as is possible."

If you marry a non-Christian, that is what will happen with you. Do not think that you will lift the non-Christian up, and that he will become a Christian. That may happen eventually because of God's great grace, but even if it does, there will still be years of heartbreak and sorrow. If the person you love is not a Christian or does not become one some time before the engagement, I tell you on the authority of God's Word that he or she is not the husband or wife for you. The Bible says, "Do not be bound together with unbelievers; for what partnership have righteousness and lawlessness, or what fellowship has light with darkness?" (2 Corinthians 6:14). You will have a marriage of body with body and sometimes even of soul with soul, but you will never have a marriage of spirit with spirit. And that is what God wants your marriage to be.

When God created us male and female and established the state of marriage, He did so for a definite purpose: to provide the best illustration in life of how He joins a man or woman to Jesus Christ forever.

Someone may say, "But didn't God create marriage so there would be children? Isn't it for reproduction?"

No, it is not. I know that this is one sideline. But it is secondary. If it were not, a marriage without children would be incomplete, a failure. That is not true.

Well, then, why did God establish marriage? He established it as an illustration of the relationship between Christ and the church. Paul says in Ephesians 5 that a wife is to submit herself to her husband "as to the Lord" (v. 22). He says that a husband is to love his wife "just as Christ also loved the church and gave Himself up for her" (v. 25). He concludes by saying of marriage, "This mystery is great; but I am speaking with reference to Christ and the church" (v. 32). In other words, God established marriage so that a Christian husband and wife could act out in their own relationship the relationship that Christ has to the Christian and thereby point men to Him as the supreme lover, bridegroom, husband, protector, and provider of His church.

What is the secret to having a happy marriage then? It is not really much of a secret. First, the husband and wife must be Christians. Second, they must take their pattern for marriage from Scripture. Third, there should be no jokes about marriage. Fourth, there should be a regular sexual union. Fifth, the husband and wife must make efforts to grow together intellectually and emotionally. Sixth, they must be willing to accept the other person as he or she is. Seventh, both must seek to glorify the Lord Jesus Christ in and through the marriage relationship.

To marry as God intends men and women to marry is to illustrate the most sublime of relationships—the relationship of the Lord Jesus Christ to those who believe on Him, and the relationship of the church to Jesus, to the one who loved us and gave Himself for us. If you see this truth, then you are well on the way to a blessed and happy marriage. You have the spiritual motivation and overall orientation to make it possible.

NOTES

1. Walter A. Maier, *For Better Not For Worse* (St. Louis: Concordia, 1935), p. 18.
2. Keith Miller, *A Taste of New Wine* (Waco, Tex.: Word, 1968), p. 46.

8

How to Be Happy as a Family

One of the most important things about a Christian marriage is that, within the relationship, God has established an organic union between two persons—an organic union, not an organization. But when that is said, it must also be said that marriage does have organizational aspects. How is a marriage to function after the wedding vows are taken? Is it to be a democracy or a dictatorship? Is it to be a monarchy or a republic? What are the duties of the husband, wife, and children to each other and to the Lord?

Many questions regarding marriage can be answered from Ephesians 5:22-30. Here the apostle Paul sets forth marriage as an illustration of the relationship of Jesus Christ to the church, and it is in terms of that relationship that the duties of the husband and wife to each other are established.

The wife is to submit herself to her husband "as to the Lord." The husband is to love his wife "just as Christ also loved the church and gave Himself up for her." Later, in chapter 6, children are told to obey their parents "in the Lord; for this is right." And they are to honor their father and mother. The parents on their part, are to raise their children "in the discipline and instruction of the Lord."

Let us now look at the rules governing each of these relationships.

The first word God has is to the wives. It is an unpopular word, especially today, for God says that the wife is to "submit" herself to her husband. When my wife and I were married in June of 1962, Robert Lamont of the First Presbyterian Church of Pittsburgh performed the ceremony and spoke for a few minutes from this passage. After the ceremony, a woman came up to us and said that she had never heard those things before. We asked, "What things?" She said, "About a wife submitting to her husband," and she added that she was going to go home and tear that page out of her Bible.

What she did not know was that tearing out the fifth chapter of Ephesians would not have solved her problem, for the same teachings are found throughout the Bible. It is true that Ephesians contains the most extensive passage. It says, "Wives be subject [submit] to your own husbands, as to the Lord. For the husband is the head of the wife, as Christ also is the head of the church, He Himself being the Savior of the body. But as the church is subject to Christ, so also the wives ought to be to their husbands in everything" (Ephesians 5:22-24). But the same thing is said as far back as in Genesis 3. "To the woman He said, 'I will greatly multiply your pain in childbirth, in pain you shall bring forth children; yet your desire shall be for your husband, and he shall rule over you'" (v. 16). Colossians 3:18 says, "Wives, be subject to your husbands, as is fitting in the Lord." In 1 Peter 3:1 we read, "In the same way, you wives, be submissive to your own husbands." Again the reference is to the standards set for all of us by Christ.

I think that the biggest difficulty with those verses today is that most wives do not realize what they actually mean. And I suspect that most husbands do not understand them either. Once I was counseling a couple who were soon to be married. I asked if they understood what God meant when He said that the wife was to be in subjection to her husband and that the husband was to love his wife as Christ loved the church and gave himself for it. The wife-to-be was wise enough to remain silent. But the man blurted out, "That means we are to love each other; but whenever we disagree, I am to give her a hug and a kiss, and after that we're to do things my way." Well, if the husband thought that, it was no wonder the wife disliked the teaching. And if husbands in general misunderstand it, who can hold the wives responsible?

What does it mean that the wife is to submit herself to her husband as unto the Lord? It certainly does not mean that she is submitting to a form of slavery or tyranny. We are not called by Christ to a form of slavery or tyranny. It does not mean a type of blind obedience either, for a wife is not chattel. Neither does it mean that the submission itself is entirely one-sided, for the verse immediately before this says that we are to submit ourselves *"to one another* in the fear of Christ" (Ephesians 5:21). Actually, the verse means that the wife was created primarily as a helpmeet for the man. And thus, where necessary, she is to submit her interests to his.

The word *submit* refers to a type of obedience that is supporting—like a foundation supporting a house or a member of the White House cabinet supporting the President of the United States. The wife is to be that to her husband. If any wife is thinking to herself that that is a demeaning position, she is to remember that the same chapter of 1 Corinthians which says that the "head of the woman is the man" also says that Christ is the head of the man and that God is the head of Christ. No woman should be ashamed to be part of that relationship.

I do not think the position that God sets forth here for the woman necessarily means that the woman cannot have a large measure of independence. For instance, there is no reason why she cannot pursue a career. There are conditions in which a woman can do this and still support her husband within the marriage relationship—for instance, in order to increase the family income at the time when the children are going through college.

It does not mean that the woman cannot pursue her own interests. In fact, it is a dull marriage if the wife does not have any outside interests. However, if the two come into conflict—that is, if the wife's career hurts the career of the husband, or if her interests lessen her concern for his work and the goals he is pursuing—then the wife is to yield to him in exactly the same way she should yield if her interests come into conflict with the way marked out for her by Jesus Christ.

If someone says, "But isn't that unfair?" the answer is that it is not unfair, for that is the way God made things. Moreover, no wife will be truly happy in her marriage until she is willing to let God trim her interests wherever necessary in order to balance those of the man.

Let me add one more thing for wives before I go on. If you are to be all that God intends you to be as a wife, you must show an interest in what your husband is doing, and for that you must be informed. I know of a marriage in which the wife has never shown any interest in her husband's work; instead she has always insisted that he leave the problems of his work at the office. The result has been a sense of unfulfilled need for the husband and an increasingly limited and introverted existence for the wife. How much better it would have been if they could have grown in the man's work and responsibilities together!

Moreover, if you are to be a proper helpmeet to your husband, you must read to be well informed, and you must look attractive. Do not forget that your husband spends the better part of his day with people who are interested in his work and who are, therefore, at least partially stimulating. The persons he works with are usually making at least some effort to be attractive, particularly the women. How then is he to be excited about loving you as Christ loves the church if he comes home to find you with your hair in curlers and so taken up with household affairs that the most interesting part of your conversation has to do with enzyme active detergents or baby food? I know that you are busy. Being a housewife is often far from fun. But you must build some time into your schedule in which you can read and keep up your appearance. Read books. Read a good news magazine. Read something about his work and his hobbies. I sometimes think that time spent in this way is almost as important as time spent reading the Bible. Anyway, it is certainly more important than the time spent watching television.

All this is only one side of the relationship, of course. For if God sets a high standard before the woman, he sets an even higher standard before the man. The wife is to love her husband and submit to him as she loves Christ and submits to Christ. But the husband is to love his wife *as Christ loved* us and gave Himself for us.

Husbands, do you love your wives like that? If you do, you will find that they will have little difficulty in submitting themselves to you in the way Jesus Christ intended. There is an incident in one of the Greek histories that illustrates this point exactly. The wife of one of the generals of Cyrus, the ruler of Persia, was charged with treachery against the king. After a trial, she was condemned to die. At first her husband did not realize what had taken place. When he was told about it, he at once burst into the throne room. He threw himself on the floor before the king and cried, "O lord, take my life instead of hers. Let me die in her place."

Cyrus, who by all historical accounts was a noble and extremely sensitive man, was touched by this offer. He said, "Love like that must not be spoiled by death." Then he gave the husband and wife back to each other and let the wife go free.

As they walked away happily, the husband said to his wife, "Did you notice how kindly the king looked upon us when he gave you the pardon?"

The wife replied, "I had no eyes for the king. I saw only the man who was willing to die in my place."

That is the picture the Holy Spirit paints for us in Ephesians 5. The husband is to love his wife as Christ loved the church. Most wives will have little difficulty in obeying a man who is willing to be crucified for them.

Another aspect of this relationship is that the husband is not to criticize his wife publicly. In fact, he is to be her shield and intercessor. The Bible says that Christ gave Himself for the church, not that He might criticize it, but "that He might *sanctify* her, having *cleansed* her by the washing of water with the word; that He might present to Himself the church in all her glory, having no spot or wrinkle or any such thing; but that she should be holy and blameless. So *husbands ought also to love their own wives*" (Ephesians 5:26-28, italics added). To listen to some husbands talk, you would think that those verses were never in the Bible. Yet they are, and they mean that, if you are a husband, God holds you responsible for the defense of your wife and, to some degree also, for her spiritual growth and understanding.

An equally important verse for husbands is 1 Peter 3:7 which says, "You husbands likewise, live with your wives in an understanding way, as with a weaker vessel, since she is a woman; and grant her honor as a fellow heir of the grace of life, so that your prayers may not be hindered." Simply put, that means that God will not even hear the prayers of a man who is too ignorant to know how to treat his wife or too foolish to value her as the greatest gift God has for him on this earth.

What does it mean to dwell with a wife in an understanding way? Well, for one thing, it means to do those little things for her that do not mean much to you but that are everything to a woman. Keith Miller said that for him dwelling with his wife according to knowledge meant learning to empty the trash basket for her. And it was not easy, for he had always thought of trash baskets as "women's work." Billy Graham believes that dwelling with a wife according to knowledge also means being courteous. He has written, "You remember when you were sweethearts how courteous you were? You used to go around the car and open the door and say, 'Darling, won't you step out?' Now you don't. You remember before you were married how you used to take off your coat and put it down in the mud puddle and tell her to walk over it! Now when she comes to a mud puddle you say, 'Jump, lady, I think you can make it.' "

There might be a most astounding transformation of our

homes and our society if only men would learn to treat their wives properly.

The most important thing God commands the husband to be is the spiritual head of his home. But since that involves the children as well as the wife, I propose to treat it more broadly in that context.

What does the Bible say to children? The Bible says, "Honor your father and your mother" (Exodus 20:12). But if they are to do that, then we must be the kind of father and mother that our children can honor. The Bible says, "My son, observe the commandment of your father, and do not forsake the teaching of your mother; bind them continually on your heart; tie them around your neck" (Proverbs 6:20-21). But if God tells a son to give such meticulous attention to the instruction received from his parents, it is then implied that the parents must give sound counsel. Clearly, God holds parents—and particularly fathers—responsible for the spiritual life of their homes.

There must be daily Bible reading in which all members of the family are involved. Thanks should be said before meals. The family must worship together. Fathers, do not claim that your home is a Christian home if those elements are missing. The individuals themselves may be Christians. But the home is not a Christian home unless those who are members of it worship, study the Bible, and pray together.

The Bible teaches that children are to obey their parents. If they do not, the parent is responsible before God to establish discipline and mete out punishment. Someone may say, "Do you mean that the Bible tells me to spank my children?" Yes, I do. The Bible says, "Chasten thy son while there is hope, and let not thy soul spare for his crying" (Proverbs 19:18, KJV). "Do not hold back discipline from the child, although you beat him with the rod, he will not die" (Proverbs 23:13). "He who spares his rod hates his son, but he who loves him disciplines him diligently" (Proverbs 13:24). "Foolishness is bound up in the heart of a child; the rod of discipline will remove it far from him" (Proverbs 22:15). That is the Bible. That is God speaking.

A woman once came to Billy Graham and said, "Mr. Graham, don't you think that all my little boy needs is a pat on the back?" Graham answered, "Lady, if it is low enough and hard enough, it will be all right."

I know quite well that each child is different and requires different handling. Some children do not need to be spanked in order to be disciplined. For some a sharp word is sufficient. The principle, however, is that discipline must be established and maintained, and when the parent is disobeyed, there must be chastisement. What is more, there must be chastisement within the general spiritual life and worshipful atmosphere of the home.

We have touched on many things in this study of the home, but they will be of little effect unless each of us will put them into practical use.

Some of what I have been saying will apply to those who are not married but who are thinking about it. You must hold these great standards of marriage up before you and evaluate the one you are thinking of marrying in the light of them. Girls, you must look at that fellow and ask, "Can he be as Jesus Christ to me? Can he be for me a man whom I can obey and to whom I can submit, subordinating many of my interests to his?" If you cannot, look elsewhere. You fellows must say, "Am I willing to give of myself for her? Do I love her enough and respect her enough to die for her? Am I willing to be patient with her and even to cover up her faults as God instructs me to?" If you cannot say those things, then it is not right for you to marry her.

Some will be beyond the stage of courtship and the early years of marriage and will be facing problems with raising their children. You must not let the difficulties you encounter deter you from the true course of action. Your children may be stubborn, but the Bible does not promise that they will be docile. That is why you may have to spank them. It is possible that they do not even respond to the spanking. Do not give up on that account. Keep at it. Isaiah wrote that God's methods with us are "precept . . . upon precept, precept upon precept: line upon line, line upon line; here a little, and there a little" (Isaiah 28:10, KJV);

His methods must be ours. Moreover, you must pray for your children and ask God to create in you the kind of character that will be winsome and that your children can respect.

Finally, there will be some for whom these words seem too late. In your case love has died, and there seems to be nothing that will rescue your marriage from that void. If it were not for what your friends would think of you, you would proceed with a divorce. What should you do? You must yield to the Lord Jesus Christ and let Him rekindle a love that has grown cold or resurrect a love that has died.

A woman once told me that at one point in her marriage her love had died entirely; she had come to hate her husband so much she could have stabbed him with a knife. But as she yielded to Christ and grew in Him, that love was rekindled, and she learned that Jesus is indeed able to bring life out of death, love out of hate, and a true Christian marriage out of sham and hostility.

If you will yield to Christ and His standards, He will begin by making you a new creation and end by making all things new.

9

How to Defeat Temptation

Most of us have heard scores of jokes about temptation, such as those by Oscar Wilde, who wrote in *The Picture of Dorian Gray,* "The only way to get rid of a temptation is to yield to it"; and in *Lady Windermere's Fan,* "I can resist anything... except temptation."

Jokes such as these are thought to be funny by those who are not engaged in the struggle. But any who are seriously struggling with temptation know that temptation is real, that it is serious, and that it can come to any believer in the Lord Jesus Christ, from any quarter, at any time.

A serious writer wrote, "The source of temptation is in man himself." Another declared, "The temptation is not here, where you are reading about it or praying about it. It is down in your shop, among bales and boxes, tenpenny nails, and sandpaper."

What should be our attitude to temptation? Should we cower before it or run from it? Should we submit or resist? The biblical answers to those questions teach us that we should resist. And they assure us that God is indeed able to help and deliver those who are tempted. The author of Hebrews said of Jesus Christ,

"He had to be made like His brethren in all things, that He might become a merciful and faithful high priest in things pertaining to God, to make propitiation for the sins of the people. For since He Himself was tempted in that which He has suffered, *He is able to come to the aid of those who are tempted*" (Hebrews 2:17-18, italics added).

What is temptation? The clearest answer to that question comes from the book of James. The author wrote, "Consider it all joy, my brethren, when you encounter various trials [KJV, temptations], knowing that the testing of your faith produces endurance" (James 1:2-3). In those verses it is obvious that James was referring to a kind of temptation that comes to a Christian from God and that is intended by God for the strengthening of the Christian's faith and character. That is the kind of testing that came to Abraham when God asked him to sacrifice his son Isaac. It was not a temptation to sin. It was a test of whether or not he would believe and trust God. When he did trust God, he grew. Clearly we are not to pray to escape that type of temptation but rather should receive it willingly, as James said. We can do that when we are afflicted by any form of suffering, persecution, discouragement, or abuse for the cause of Christ.

Several verses farther on in the chapter, James wrote of a temptation that is not from God. This is temptation in a second sense of the word, and it is not at all desirable. "Let no one say when he is tempted, 'I am being tempted by God'; for God cannot be tempted by evil, and He Himself does not tempt anyone. But each one is tempted when he is carried away and enticed by his own lust" (James 1:13-14). This verse identifies man himself as one source of that type of temptation.

The last verse of the chapter speaks of a Christian's duty to keep himself "unstained by the world" (James 1:27). Hence, it would seem that the world is a source of temptation also.

Finally, in chapter 4, verse 7, James spoke of the assaults we receive from the devil. He said, "Submit therefore to God. Resist the devil and he will flee from you."

How to Defeat Temptation

When we summarize those verses, we see that there are two basic kinds of temptation—temptations from God, which are good, and temptations to sin, which are evil. The second kind of temptation, temptation to sin, may be divided into temptations of the flesh, the world, and Satan. It is over those temptations that every believer must triumph.

But how do we triumph over the temptations that come to us from the world, the flesh, and the devil? How are we to defeat those temptations?

We should begin with fleshly temptations, since you and I generally think of them first. What are they? Quite obviously they are at least temptations to sexual sins, drunkenness, overeating, pampering of our bodies, and so on. But we cannot limit the sins of the flesh to those things. What about laziness, for instance? Shouldn't fleshly sins include the desire to stay home and enjoy comfort, while others are suffering great material deprivation or are working hard? Shouldn't they include the temptation to buy the second car, take the long vacation, or whatever it may be (all perfectly legitimate things in themselves), when we could help important spiritual enterprises by our giving or by a better use of our time? Aren't they also the temptations to stay home on week nights and watch television, when we know of a need for tutoring the underprivileged, befriending the lonely, or visiting the sick?

How are we to defeat those temptations? There is only one answer according to the Word of God. We are to run from them. We are to remove ourselves from the place of temptation. That was Paul's advice to his converts in reference to sexual sins. He advised the Corinthians, "Flee immorality" (1 Corinthians 6:18). He told the young man Timothy, "Now flee from youthful lusts, and pursue righteousness, faith, love, and peace, with those who call on the Lord from a pure heart" (2 Timothy 2:22). In other words, in reference to sexual sins, imitate Joseph, who fled from Potiphar's wife, and not David, who invited Bathsheba over to the palace.

A moment's reflection will show why in some instances that

must be so. In most of the temptations of this life, although they may be severe, the Christian has an ally in reason. For example, he may be tempted to cheat on his income tax, but his reason will tell him that the computers today are very thorough and that the gain (if there is any) is entirely out of proportion to the loss of money, time, and reputation if he should be caught. Reason unites with his knowledge of the good and the internal witness of the Holy Spirit to save him. It is the same with many other temptations, but not with most of the fleshly temptations. What couple ever sat alone in an apartment reasoning out the relative advantages and disadvantages of premarital sex, for instance, and on that basis either had sexual intercourse or avoided it?

It does not work that way. Consequently, if you find yourself in that situation, you must start running, like Joseph. Get out of the apartment. Go to a restaurant. Visit a friend. If your problem is drunkenness, you must avoid bars. If it is overeating, you must force yourself away from the table. If you are lazy, turn off the television set. Without such aid neither you nor anyone else is 100 percent able at all times to avoid those temptations.

The second main source of temptations is the world. What is the world? Clearly the Bible is not talking about the physical earth when it speaks of the world's temptations. It is talking about a system of values that are not divine values and about a way of life that is not God's way of life. The Oxford English Dictionary hits upon this sense of the word when it defines the world as "worldly affairs, the aggregate of things earthly." In this area we must place temptations to become president of the company or of the woman's auxiliary at the expense of others who also want the top position. We must include most of the sins of pride—pride in our ancestry, our wealth, our "superior" taste in art, music, or drama. We must include all desires to "put down" other people.

Is there a specific biblical cure for those temptations? Yes, there is. But, unfortunately, in this area the solution is not so quick or so simple as with the sins of the flesh. This cure is gradual. Paul spoke of it when he said, "I urge you therefore,

How to Defeat Temptation

brethren, by the mercies of God, to present your bodies a living and holy sacrifice, acceptable to God, which is your spiritual service of worship. And do not be conformed to this world, but be transformed by the renewing of your mind, that you may prove what the will of God is, that which is good and acceptable and perfect" (Romans 12:1-2). That means that we are to overcome the world's temptations by allowing God to transform us from within into Christ's image. That He will do as we surrender our wills to His will and begin to walk in the path He sets before us.

The final type of temptation is that which comes to us from the devil. The secret to resisting that type of temptation is found in James 4:7, which we quoted earlier. We have seen that the temptation that comes from the flesh is to be resisted by *fleeing* from it (1 Corinthians 6:18; 2 Timothy 2:22). We are to resist the temptation that comes to us from the world by allowing God to *transform* us by the renewing of our minds, that we may prove His perfect will for us (Romans 12:1-2). But when it comes to the devil, Scripture says, *"Submit* therefore to God. *Resist* the devil and he will flee from you" (James 4:7, italics added).

At this point we must be very clear about what James was saying. He said, "Submit to God" and "resist the devil." We are to *submit* and *resist*. But how can we do that? What does submission mean? And how can we resist the wisdom and superior cunning of Satan? We need to answer those questions clearly, for if we are sensitive to spiritual things we know that Satan is stronger than we are. We know that we are unable to resist him in ourselves and that we are weak beside him. Therefore, we need to know how we are to seek deliverance through the one who Himself defeated Satan.

What does it mean to submit? Quite simply, it means to surrender one's will to God. And since that cannot be done in isolation apart from a personal relationship to Him, it means that we must spend time conversing with God through prayer. It is certainly no accident, for instance, that in the Lord's Prayer the petition "Do not lead us into temptation, but deliver us from evil," comes last, after the Christian has already prayed, "Hallowed be Thy name. Thy kingdom come. Thy will be done." That means that although the believer is to resist the devil, although he is to fight against him, he is able to do that successfully only after he has first of all submitted himself to God.

What does it mean to resist? How do we resist? The answer is: by means of God's Word. The Lord Jesus Christ said to His disciples, "You are already clean because of the word which I have spoken to you" (John 15:3), meaning that purity of life can be ours to the degree that we feed upon the Bible and study it. The psalmist said, "How can a young man keep his way pure? By keeping it according to Thy word. . . . Thy word I have treasured in my heart, that I may not sin against Thee" (Psalm 119:9, 11). Paul, writing specifically of our spiritual warfare against Satan, said, "And take . . . the sword of the Spirit, which is the word of God" (Eph. 6:17).

The greatest example of successful warfare against Satan is the victory over him by the Lord Jesus Christ, as recorded in Matthew 4:1-11. It illustrates many of the points we have been making. We must not think that that was the only occasion in Christ's life when the Lord Jesus Christ was tempted. He was "tempted in all things as we are," and that would involve prolonged and continuing temptation, as well as those brief encounters. Nevertheless, those are perhaps His most significant temptations, and they are certainly included in the Bible to teach us the means of victory over them.

Some time ago I was on this subject in connection with a series of studies on the Sermon on the Mount for The Bible Study Hour. Walt Teas, the announcer, asked me during a question-and-answer period: "We have all heard the expression that temptations come to us from the world, the flesh, and the devil, but it seems that all three of Christ's temptations came to Him from the devil. If that is right, how can we say that Jesus 'was in in points tempted like as we are, yet without sin' [Hebrews 4:15, KJV]?"

It was a good question. I pointed out that there is a fine distinction here on the basis of which it was necessary for Jesus to be tempted in all points directly by the devil. Jesus did not have a sinful nature as we do, so He could not be tempted by a sinful nature. Neither could He be tempted by the world directly because the sins of the world are pride, arrogance, a desire for dominance, and so on, and Jesus had no point of contact in Himself for those. If Jesus was to be tempted at all, all the temptations must have had to come to Him from a direct encounter with the devil, just as Adam and Eve had to receive their temptations from the devil. Before their Fall, Adam and Eve did not have a sinful nature either.

At the same time, however, we notice as we read the account of Christ's temptations that each of the temptations did relate to one of those three areas. The temptation to turn stones into bread was a fleshly temptation; the temptation to throw Himself from the top of the Temple in Jerusalem was a temptation to gain the world's esteem in the world's way; the temptation to worship Satan was an outright spiritual temptation that would have placed the Lord in opposition to His heavenly Father. Thus, although all the temptations came originally from the devil, they were nevertheless temptations to the sins of the flesh, the world, and the devil. And they show us that Jesus was tempted in all ways as we are. Of course, because of their source, those temptations were far stronger and more subtle than our temptations.

How did the Lord Jesus Christ come out on top of those temptations? The answer to that question is contrary to what most people think, for they think that He did it by drawing on His divine nature. They believe that He had more power to resist temptation than we do. It is true, of course, that Jesus did have more power than we do. But there is nothing in the Bible to show that Christ ever resisted temptation by drawing on His divine nature. Jesus was both man and God. Yet He resisted temptation as a man. What is more, it is for that reason that He is an example for us when we are tempted.

So let me ask the question again: How did Jesus resist the

temptations that are recorded in Matthew 4? First, He had just spent forty days in fasting and in prayer. Second, He replied to the devil in every instance by quoting Scripture.

Satan had come to Him saying, "If You are the Son of God, command that these stones become bread" (v. 3). That was a temptation to put physical needs above spiritual ones, and Jesus answered by saying, "MAN SHALL NOT LIVE ON BREAD ALONE, BUT ON EVERY WORD THAT PROCEEDS OUT OF THE MOUTH OF GOD" (v. 4). That is a direct quotation from Deuteronomy 8:3. Next the devil took Him up to Jerusalem and, placing Him on a pinnacle of the Temple, challenged Him to throw Himself down, trusting God to bear Him up. In that way Christ would appear to be coming from heaven and thereby gain an immediate following. Jesus answered by quoting Deuteronomy 6:16, "It is written, 'YOU SHALL NOT TEMPT THE LORD YOUR GOD'" (Matthew 4:7). In the final temptation Satan asked Christ to worship him in exchange for this world's glory. That was a spiritual temptation. Jesus replied, "Begone, Satan! For it is written, 'YOU SHALL WORSHIP THE LORD YOUR GOD, AND SERVE HIM ONLY'" (v. 10). Once again Jesus resisted the devil, with a quotation from Deuteronomy 6:13.

Jesus overcame temptation from the devil just as we are to overcome it—by prayer and knowledge of the Bible. Certainly when we learn to pray as Jesus prayed, and when we know the Bible as Jesus knew the Bible, then we will experience victory over our temptations also.

Moreover, if we do those things, we will also have great confidence before God, even when we are faced with temptations. We will pray that God will keep us from temptation, knowing that "God is faithful, who will not allow you to be tempted beyond what you are able, but with the temptation will provide the way of escape also, that you may be able to endure it" (1 Corinthians 10:13).

10

How to Overcome Anger

Some time ago I heard of a man who claimed that he never got angry. He had a very bad temper. But when someone confronted him with the fact that he often did get angry, even though he claimed he did not, the man replied, "I am never angry as long as I get what I want." Unfortunately, he failed to recognize that he had a serious personal problem and, therefore, failed to look for a solution.

That might not have been the case if he had only realized how serious anger is. Psychologists tell us that anger, particularly anger that is buried inside, is destructive and is quite capable of ruining a life that otherwise would be healthy and productive. The Lord Jesus Christ said the same thing when discussing the real meaning of the sixth commandment. The sixth commandment, which had been known to Israel for centuries, says, "Thou shalt not kill [KJV]"—meaning murder. But "murder" was described by most religious leaders in Israel as only the external act. They had taken the sixth commandment as found in Exodus 20:13, and had combined it with Numbers 35:30, which demanded death for anyone who unlawfully took innocent life.

They thereby implied that the commandment referred to nothing more or less than that act.

We do the same thing, of course, for our dictionaries define murder as the "offense of unlawfully killing a human being with malice aforethought, express or implied."

Is murder nothing more than an act? Is there no guilt in the man who almost kills another but is prevented from doing so only by some unexpected circumstance? What about the man who is afraid to kill but who "murders" his enemy with invective?

God did not intend the sixth commandment to have such a limited meaning. Therefore Jesus said that God looks at the heart and that He is as much concerned with unjustified anger as with the actual shedding of blood. He told His followers, "You have heard that the ancients were told, 'You shall not commit murder' and 'Whosoever commits murder shall be liable to the court.' But I say to you that every one who is angry with his brother shall be guilty before the court" (Matthew 5:21-22).

Nor is that all. Not only is unjustified anger forbidden, but, according to Jesus, God will not even excuse a person who is guilty of expressions of contempt. He continued, "Whoever shall say to his brother, 'Raca,' shall be guilty before the supreme court; and whoever shall say, 'You fool,' shall be guilty enough to go into firey hell" (v. 22). *Raca* is a term meaning "empty"; but the insult is more in the sound than the meaning. Its most concrete meaning would be "a nobody." A good contemporary parallel would be "boy" when spoken derogatively. *Moros*, which is translated "fool," really means one who plays the fool morally. Hence this word is a slur on one's reputation.

Obviously such a definition of murder searches to the depth of our beings and to the things that we say when we are angry. There is a difference between righteous anger and unrighteous anger. Jesus Himself spoke in righteous anger against the hypocritical stand taken by the so-called leaders of His day. There is also a difference between impatience and the vilification of another verbally. But it is not very often that our anger is righteous, nor does it generally stop with our being impatient.

Do we commit murder? Yes, we do, according to this definition. We lose our tempers. We harbor grudges. We gossip. We kill by neglect, spite, and jealousy. Besides, if only we could see our hearts as God is able to see them, we no doubt would realize that we actually do worse things. It is no accident that, even in our own speech, such things sometimes are termed character assassination or that we speak of destroying a person by words. That is literally true, but Jesus said that, as Christians, we are to overcome anger.

Those verses go on to show in a far more positive way what the cure for anger is. The first step in that cure, according to Jesus, is to *admit that we do get angry*. We must recognize the fault first of all.

One would think that such a point would be obvious, and that anyone would do so naturally. But it is not obvious, even though modern psychiatry teaches the same thing. The subtlety of the human mind prevents it. A man can do the worst possible things—kill, cheat, steal, commit adultery, and so on. But when he is brought face to face with his actions, he will find a dozen reasons why those were not wrong at all, or why it was necessary for him to do them. We sin, but we cover up the sin. We refuse to acknowledge it even to ourselves. No wonder, then, that Jesus taught we are to acknowledge our anger first of all.

The second step for those who wish to overcome their anger is to *correct the injustice,* for there is always injustice on both sides in any normal dispute. Thus Jesus said, "If therefore you are presenting your offering at the altar, and there remember that your brother has something against you, leave your offering there before the altar, and go your way; first be reconciled to your brother, and then come and present your offering" (Matthew 5:23-24).

Someone might ask at this point, "But didn't the sacrifice atone for sin and cover the guilt of the one presenting it?" Yes, but it never excused the necessity for restitution. Remember that King David was saved and is in heaven today because he looked for the Messiah, who he knew was coming to save men from their sin. But when he wrote of his daily relationship to God and of his sin, David said, "If I regard wickedness in my heart, the Lord will not hear" (Psalm 66:18). On the occasion of Saul's first great disobedience to the Lord after he was king, Samuel said to him, "Has the LORD as much delight in burnt offerings and sacrifices as in obeying the voice of the LORD? Behold, to obey is better than sacrifice, and to heed than the fat of rams" (1 Samuel 15:22).

Today, too, men find it easier to substitute the ceremonial aspects of religion for the demands of a clear conscience before God. Whereas in ancient times that meant the presentation of sacrifices at the Temple in Jerusalem, today it means the attendance of a Christian at church, his participation in a Bible study or prayer meeting, or his giving to the church or missionaries. Those things are right in themselves. We should do them. But God says that they are worthless from His point of view as long as there is unconfessed sin in the life of the Christian and failure on the Christian's part to make things right. John wrote, "Little children, let us not love with word or with tongue, but in deed and truth. . . . in whatever our heart condemns us; for God is greater than our heart, and knows all things" (1 John 3:18, 20). Consequently, we should confess those things and make them right insofar as we are able.

The third step in Christ's cure for anger is to *do what we must do, immediately.* That is the point of the next two verses of this chapter, for Jesus spoke of agreeing with your adversary quickly lest the most terrible consequences follow. These verses do not teach, as some suppose, that God is the adversary and that we can lose our salvation if we continue in a course marked out for us by anger. Jesus did not mean that. Actually, He was saying that sin has consequences and that, if you want to avoid the consequences, you should confess and make right the sin as soon as you are able. In this sense the Lord was only saying in different words what Paul later said to the Ephesians, "Be angry, and yet do not sin; do not let the sun go down on your anger" (Ephesians 4:26). Jesus was recognizing the great principle stated in the book of Hebrews, "Pursue peace with all men, and . . . sanctification . . . that no root of bitterness springing up causes trouble, and by it many be defiled" (Hebrews 12:14-15).

A fourth step in the cure of anger must be added to those three obvious steps on the basis of all that Christ is saying. It is that we must *ask God to change our heart,* because only God is able to do it.

One Sunday evening I was talking with one of my daughters and learned that she was greatly offended because she thought someone had mistreated her. He had held her upside down, and she did not like that and was angry about it. She said to me, "I don't like that man; I'm never going to forgive him. I'll forgive Cici, and Vicky, and Pamela [her friends], but not him." I said, "Oh, you don't want to say that. Jesus tells us that we are supposed to forgive one another; He forgives us, doesn't He?" She said, "Yes, I know. They teach me that in Sunday school and at school, but I don't understand it. What I'd really like to do is kick him." I said, "Yes, that's the way we are. But God wants us to be different."

If you honestly look into your own heart when you are offended, you will find that what you would most like to do is to kick the person. It is often what I would most like to do. And yet, you must not do it. In fact, you must even come to the point at which you ask God to change your heart and mind so that you do not even want to do it. If you ask, God will change your mind—we will be transformed from within by the renewing of our minds (Romans 12:2)—and you will find it possible to do what beforehand you judged impossible.

Moreover, this will be possible for you even if the other person does not return the favor and maintains a white-hot anger against you. Paul wrote, "Never take your own revenge, beloved, but leave room for the wrath of God, for it is written, 'Vengeance is Mine, I will repay,' says the Lord. But if your enemy is hungry, feed him, and if he is thirsty, give him a drink; for in so doing you will heap burning coals upon his head. Do not be overcome by evil, but overcome evil with good" (Romans 12:19-21). Paul was saying that we should not retaliate against wrong done to ourselves, but step aside and let the wrath of men work, even to our harm. If you should be saying, "But they will harm me," the answer is "Vengeance is Mine, I will repay, says the Lord." In other words, God says that if we live as He intends us to live, men will become angry with us, but He Himself promises to protect our interests. We may not see how they are protected until we get to heaven. But we will get to heaven, and there those who lived as Christ lived will be vindicated.

"Do not be overcome by evil, but overcome evil with good." It is a difficult statement to accept. In fact, it is an impossible statement if the heart of man is unchanged. But God will change your heart if you surrender your life to Jesus Christ and ask Him to transform it.

11

How to Be Free From Worry

Some time ago a popular magazine published an article on the presence of worry in America. The point of the study was this: The breakdown of faith in God and in reason, coupled with the accelerated pace and high tension of modern life, has produced intense anxiety in many millions of people, so much so in fact that it is correct to call worry one of the most widespread and debilitating characteristics of our time.

The article said that not just "the black statistics of murder, suicide, alcoholism, and divorce betray anxiety . . . but almost any innocent everyday act: the limp or overhearty handshake, the second pack of cigarettes or the third martini . . . the stammer in mid-sentence, the wasted hour before the TV set, the spanked child." The writers added that those symptoms are intensified for many of us by the dominant American myths that "the old can grow young, the indecisive can become leaders of men, the housewives can become glamour girls . . . the slow-witted can become intellectuals."[1]

In that analysis the magazine was, I believe, at its best. For it is true that worry *is* with us and that millions of persons (many of them Christians) are troubled by it. Worry is not well defined. Perhaps the very vagueness of worry is its worst feature. Someone has called anxiety "fear in search of a cause." Kierkegaard once wrote, "No Grand Inquisitor has in readiness such terrible tortures as anxiety."

Is there a cure for anxiety? The only solutions that the magazine article offered were sedatives and psychiatry. Fortunately, the Bible offers an entirely different and far more effective cure for Christians.

At this point some may be thinking, "Do you mean to tell me that Christians, who have been saved from sin and who have come to know the Lord Jesus Christ as their Lord, can experience the same type of worry you are describing?" The answer is: Not only can Christians worry; all of us do at times, and many worry constantly.

Jesus (who knows what is in man) was aware that this is true. Therefore, in the list of warnings that begins in the middle of the Sermon on the Mount, He emphasized anxiety more than any other personal failure. He said, "For this reason I say to you, do not be anxious for your life, as to what you shall eat, or what you shall drink; nor for your body, as to what you shall put on . . . For all these things the Gentiles eagerly seek; for your heavenly Father knows that you need all these things. But seek first His kingdom and His righteousness; and all these things shall be added to you" (Matthew 6:25, 32-33).

I am glad that the translators of the *New American Standard Bible* (as well as the translators of most modern versions) did not retain the old King James expressions in this passage. The King James Bible says, "Take no thought for your life. . . . Take no thought for the morrow." That translation has misled some people into thinking that Jesus was warning against making proper provision for the future. Actually, we have a case here where words have just changed their meaning. The original, both in the Greek and the English of the time of King James, was just "stop worrying." Paul meant the same thing when he told the Philippians, "Be anxious for nothing" (Philippians

4:6). Peter was referring to the tendency of some Christians to worry when he wrote, "Casting all your anxiety upon Him, because He cares for you" (1 Peter 5:7). Christians are not to be anxious or worried about anything. We worry, but we do not need to. Moreover, we should not worry, for worry can effectively stifle the Christian life and ruin one's witness.

If we are to understand the essential point of those verses in Matthew 6, it is very important to recognize the clear outline that is here. The clue to it is found in the repetition of the word *therefore* (KJV) in verses 25, 31, and 34. It has been said that whenever in your reading of the Bible you come upon the word *therefore,* you should not go on until you understand what it is "there for." If that is true for one instance of the word, it is much truer when the word is repeated several times over.

"Therefore" really means "for this reason" or "because of this." So we immediately recognize that in those verses Jesus gives a conclusion—in each case identical—based on three things that have gone before. Because of the teaching in verse 24, the Christian is not to worry. Because of the truths in verses 26 through 30, the Christian is not to worry. Finally, because of the teaching in verses 32 and 33, the Christian is not to worry. The entire section contains three points which, in each case, are followed by the identical conclusion.

What are those three teachings? The first concerns the proper attitude of a Christian toward money. In that section of the sermon Jesus taught that the love of money is harmful because it is impossible for a person to serve God and money at the same time. Then He added that, for the same reason, His followers should not be anxious about some future happening or provision. We cannot serve God and worry at the same time.

We can see that truth in two ways. First, remember the Westminster Shorter Catechism, which says, "Man's chief end is to glorify God and to enjoy Him for ever." If that is an accurate description of our Christian service, then it is evident that we cannot serve God by glorifying Him if we are constantly filled with doubt about His ability to take care of us.

The other way to understand Christ's first point is by the old saying, "If you're worrying, you're not trusting; and if you're trusting, you're not worrying." That is literally true. It is a proper restatement of Christ's argument that you cannot serve God and keep on worrying at the same time. One commentator has written, "This recognizes the habitual attitude of the unsaved heart [he could have said of many Christian hearts, too] toward the problems and difficulties of life. God commands us to 'Stop perpetually worrying about even one thing.' We commit sin when we worry. We do not trust God when we worry. We do not receive answers to prayer when we worry, because we are not trusting."[2]

The second reason that we are not to worry involves knowledge. It is a reminder of a fact that every Christian should know—the fact that God is both able and willing to care for those who trust Him. Jesus said, "Look at the birds of the air, that they do not sow, neither do they reap, nor gather into barns, and yet your heavenly Father feeds them. Are you not worth much more than they? . . . And why are you anxious about clothing? Observe how the lilies of the field grow; they do not toil nor do they spin, yet I say to you that even Solomon in all his glory did not clothe himself like one of these. But if God so arrays the grass of the field, which is alive today and tomorrow is thrown into the furnace, will He not much more do so for you, O men of little faith?" (Matthew 6:26, 28-30).

Do you see the importance of those verses? It is not merely that we are commanded not to worry. We are given reasons why we should not worry. The command not to worry is based upon the demonstrable ability of God to take care of us.

Peter is one of many Christians who have learned this lesson. In the early days of his association with Jesus, he was worried about many things. After he first had courage to walk upon the water, he began to look at the waves and became so worried that he began to sink (Matthew 14:30). He was worried that Jesus might not pay taxes (Matthew 17:24-27). At one point he was anxious about who might betray Jesus (John 13:24).

How to Be Free From Worry

He was worried that Jesus might have to suffer, and so he rebuked Him on one occasion (Matthew 16:22) and sought to defend Him with a sword on another (John 18:10). Peter was a great worrier. But after he came to know Jesus better, he learned that Jesus was able to take care of him. Thus, toward the end of his life, he wrote to other Christians, telling them that they were to live by "casting all your anxiety upon Him, because He cares for you" (1 Peter 5:7).

In this verse the word *anxiety* is the same word as we have in the Sermon on the Mount. The word *cast* is not the normal word for throwing something. It is a word that signifies a definite act of the will by which we stop worrying about things and let God assume the responsibility for our welfare. Finally, the word *care* in the phrase "He cares for you" literally means, "for He is mindful of you and your interests." God thinks about you! That is what Peter meant. That is what God encourages you to learn also.

The final reason not to worry that Jesus gave is one that appeals to experience. Jesus said, "But seek first His kingdom and His righteousness; and all these things shall be added to you" (Matthew 6:33). In other words, make it your business to seek God's interests and follow His way and you will see that all your physical needs will be met effortlessly and without any need for you to take thought about them.

Do you know the bliss of that statement? Do you know its truth? If you do not, it may be that you have never had that hunger and thirst after righteousness that Jesus spoke of earlier in the sermon, nor the poverty of spirit that Jesus asked for in those who should inherit God's kingdom. Remember Christ's teaching recorded just a few verses earlier: "Do not lay up for yourselves treasures upon earth, where moth and rust destroy, and where thieves break in and steal. But lay up for yourselves treasures in heaven, where neither moth nor rust destroys, and where thieves do not break in or steal; for where your treasure is, there will your heart be also" (vv. 19-21).

At this point someone may be saying, "I can see from the

reasons you have been giving that I should not worry. But still I do worry. Is there an answer? What is the solution for me personally?"

I believe the answer to that question is a simple one. First, you must recognize that all the promises Christ has made in the Sermon on the Mount are for Christians only. If you are not a Christian or are uncertain as to whether you are a Christian or not, you must begin by straightening that out. Every so often someone says to me, "If God has promised to take care of all our needs, how come there is so much poverty and deprivation in the world?" The answer is that the promises of God's care are for Christian people only. They are for those who have accepted the death and resurrection of Jesus Christ as the one sufficient ground for their salvation. If you do not believe those things, then the promises of God's care are not for you.

Second, if you are a believer, you need to add to your initial experience of salvation all you can learn about God's nature and His ability to take care of His people. I begin most Sunday morning worship services in my church with a passage that teaches this exactly: "Come to Me, all who are weary and heavy-laden, and I will give you rest. Take My yoke upon you, and learn from Me, for I am gentle and humble in heart; and YOU SHALL FIND REST FOR YOUR SOULS. For My yoke is easy, and My load is light" (Matthew 11:28-30). In other words, you are to learn all you can about Jesus Christ. As you learn about Him, you will grow strong in faith, knowing that He is able to do the things He has promised.

Finally, you need to get in the habit of turning to God whenever you feel worry approaching. Your reaction in trouble should be something like a conditioned reflex. You know what a normal reflex is. If your hand accidentally touches a hot stove, your body will jerk the hand back. You do not need to think about it. It comes naturally. A conditioned reflex is the same, except that it needs to be learned. A conditioned reflex may be illustrated by the reaction you have in stepping on the brake when you see a red light or in rising to your feet when someone begins to play the "Star-Spangled Banner." Those reactions are almost automatic, but they do not result from instinct. They result from training or practice. In the same way, we need reflexes that will turn us to the Lord at the first sign of trouble.

Most persons have reactions of one sort or another. Some persons turn in upon themselves when they see trouble approaching. Others turn to some other person. Your task, as a Christian, is to supplant those or any other reactions with a behavioral pattern that turns you toward God. If you do not turn to God, you will worry. If you do turn to God, you will increasingly come to know that divine tranquility that passes all understanding and that is able to give you peace even in a time of great trouble.

In one of the early Greek manuscripts from the first centuries of the Christian era, there is a record of a man named Titedios Amerimnos. The first part of that name is a proper name. But the second part is made up of the Greek word for "worry" plus the prefix meaning "not" or "never." In other words, the second name is a descriptive epithet like the second part of Frederick the Great or James the Just. Many have thought that this man, as a pagan, constantly worried. But after he became a Christian, he stopped worrying. He was then called Titedios Amerimnos—Titedios, the Man Who Never Worries. You should be able to add that statement to your name. You should be able to write "John Smith," "Betty Jones," "Charles Miller," "Susan Moore" (or whatever it may be) and then add, "The One Who Never Worries."

NOTES

1. "The Age of Anxiety," *Time*, 31 March 1961, pp. 44, 46.
2. Kenneth S. Wuest, *Word Studies from the Greek New Testament*, 16 vols. (Grand Rapids: Eerdmans, 1966), 4:43.

12

How to Triumph in Suffering

I frequently visit a woman who has been confined to a nursing home for many years. She has a form of acute, crippling arthritis that has left her unable to walk or even to move freely. She is unable to care for herself in many simple but necessary things. At times she is in almost unbearable pain. Still she speaks of the goodness and grace of God, not only to herself, but also to many others who are with her in that home. She knows real joy, and she shows it in the midst of suffering.

I once visited a man who was in the hospital with a serious coronary thrombosis. Instead of complaining about his condition, about the medical service, or some similar thing, he was thinking of all that the Lord had done for him in past days. He was praying for those who were with him in the same room of the hospital. That man knew what it meant to rejoice always in the Lord. Both he and my other friend are exercising a supernatural joy that is their birthright as Christians.

Jesus often promised joy to those who follow Him. The angel who announced His birth to the shepherds said, "Behold, I bring you good news of a great joy which shall be for all the people;

for today in the city of David there has been born for you a Savior, who is Christ the Lord" (Luke 2:10-11). Jesus said, "These things I have spoken to you, that My joy may be in you, and that your joy may be made full" (John 15:11). In John 17 Jesus prayed to His Father "that they may have My joy made full in themselves" (John 17:13).

The possession of Christian joy in full measure is the secret of triumph in suffering. But what is joy? Quite simply, joy is a supernatural delight in God and His goodness. When joy is at work, it transforms our entire outlook on life, even its unhappy parts.

Perhaps I can better explain what joy is by contrasting it with happiness, for they are entirely different things. Every Christian attribute has its counterpart in the world. The world has passion; Christians have love. The world strives for security; Christians trust God. The world seeks self-gratification; Christians know peace, even in want. In the same way, the world seeks happiness, whereas Christians know joy.

Happiness is closely related to circumstances or chance; the word is a translation of a Latin word *fortuna,* which also means chance. Thus, if things happen to work out the way a particular individual approves, he is happy. If they do not work out that way, then he is unhappy, perhaps even miserable. Happiness is circumstantial. So, quite obviously, if we are depending upon some vague feeling of happiness to give us victory in suffering, then we will lose the battle, for our worsening circumstances will destroy it. On the other hand, joy is quite different. Joy comes directly from God and is not related to circumstances; therefore no circumstances can ever destroy it. Thus, if the individual belongs to God and is allowing God to fill him with joy— along with all the other fruits of the Christian life described in Galatians 5:22-23—he will triumph.

Unfortunately, it is impossible to speak of the supernatural qualities of Christian joy without saying at the same time that many Christians fail to experience that joy as they ought. Or they lose it after the initial joy of their salvation. Circumstances

How to Triumph in Suffering

get them down. And instead of the victory all Christians should experience, they know depression.

One of our great hymns speaks of victory even in death:

> "When through the deep waters I call thee to go,
> The rivers of sorrow shall not overflow;
> For I will be with thee, thy troubles to bless,
> And sanctify to thee thy deepest distress."

But other hymns tell of the loss of joy that is characteristic of the life of many Christians. One hymn writer wrote:

> Look how we grovel here below,
> Fond of these trifling toys;
> Our souls can neither fly nor go
> To reach eternal joys!

Another songwriter has added:

> How tedious and tasteless the hours
> When Jesus no longer I see!
> Sweet prospects, sweet birds, and sweet flowers
> Have lost their sweetness for me.

It is a sad confession. And it is doubly sad, since it is a sad state in itself and because it is true for many Christians. That should not be. Instead of depression there should be a joy in the Lord that goes beyond our circumstances.

Do you know that joy? Perhaps you are saying, "I know that I should have it, and I would like to rejoice in the Lord always. But circumstances still get me down. What can I do? How can that joy be sustained?" The answer is in God's Word, and we must follow it as we would a doctor's prescription. If you see a doctor because you feel tired and run down, and he prescribes exercise and an increase of vitamin B, you go to the drugstore and buy vitamins. And if you are disciplined, you make sure that you exercise every day. In the same way, if we lack Christian joy, we need to adhere to God's remedy.

What is that remedy? I believe God's remedy can be summed up in several principles.

The first principle is that you must be a Christian. I know that seems obvious, but in my experience at least two classes of people need to face that squarely. The first class is composed of those who are not Christians and know it, but who think that Christian fruits can be grown without a Christian life. If you are such a person, you need to recognize that joy is supernatural and that it is only given to those who have surrendered their lives to Jesus Christ.

The second class is composed of those who are not Christians but who *think* they are, perhaps because they have been raised in a religious home or because they attend church. They think they are Christians, but they do not understand the heart of the gospel and have not actually committed their lives to Jesus Christ; hence, they cannot understand their failure to experience the fruits of such commitment. If you are that kind of person, then you must begin with the first principle also.

Let me explain it as plainly as I can. Before you become a Christian, you stand before God as one who has fallen short of His standards. You come to Him with all your best traits of character. But as you stand before Him, you realize that even the best of those things is imperfect and fails before God. You hear God say, "You come to me with all that is human; but what is human is tainted by sin, and I cannot work with that. That is a foundation upon which I cannot build. You must turn from it."

And you do. You lay those things aside, you count them as loss, and you come to the cross to receive God's righteousness. You say to God, "I admit that everything I do falls short of Your standard, and I recognize Your verdict upon it. I lay it aside. I do not deserve anything from You, but I come empty-handed to receive what You have promised to give through faith in Christ Jesus. I come to receive Your righteousness, by which I am accounted righteous. I come to receive the Holy Spirit, by whom I will have power to live the Christian life. And I ask You to help me to live it for Jesus' sake. Amen."

If you have done that, you have taken the first step in experiencing the joy that is to characterize the Christian life.

The second step is this: If you are to experience God's joy, you must first know His righteousness and peace. That means that a life of holiness and trust are prerequisites. The order of those three things is set forth in Romans 14:17: "For the kingdom of God is not eating and drinking, but righteousness and peace and joy in the Holy Spirit."

Many Christians do not know the joy that could be theirs because their lives are not holy and because they do not trust God with their future. I know of one girl who would not trust God in regard to marriage. Instead of admitting that God's plan for her was best, whatever it may have been, she was intent on getting married. Her determination to get married led her into many situations that were clearly not God's will for her. They actually led her into sin. She had her way, but she was not happy. And she was the first to admit that she certainly was not experiencing God's joy.

Sin keeps us from God, who is the source of joy. And anxiety also works against it. Instead of experiencing sin and anxiety in his life, the believer in Jesus Christ should experience a life of holiness and peace. And he should realize God's peace as he submits all aspects of his future to Him. Paul wrote, "Be anxious for nothing, but in everything by prayer and supplication with thanksgiving let your requests be made known to God. And the peace of God, which surpasses all comprehension, shall guard your hearts and your minds in Christ Jesus" (Philippians 4:6-7).

The third step to a life of continuous, supernatural joy is to steep yourself in the teachings of the Bible. When I first began to study what the Bible has to say about joy, I was surprised to discover how many times joy is associated with a mature knowledge of God's Word. David said, "The precepts of the LORD are right, rejoicing the heart" (Psalm 19:8). "I have rejoiced in the way of Thy testimonies, as much as in all riches" (Psalm

119:14). Jesus said, "If you keep My commandments, you will abide in My love; just as I have kept My Father's commandments, and abide in His love. These things I have spoken to you, that My joy may be in you, and that your joy may be made full" (John 15:10-11). Those verses teach that joy is to be found in a knowledge of God's character and commandments, which can be found in His Word. If you have not known much of that joy, the reason may be a neglect of a study of Scripture.

The place that Scripture should have in your life is illustrated by an interesting custom of Old Testament times. In the days of Jesus Christ, and for hundreds of years before that, pious Jews wore on their foreheads a small device called a frontlet, which contained some words of Scripture. The frontlet was worn to remind them that God's Word was always to be the object of their deepest meditations and was to act as the source of the principles by which they ordered their lives.

The command to wear frontlets occurs three times in the Old Testament, and in each case the practice is related to one of the cardinal doctrines of Scripture.

The first mention of this custom is in Exodus 13. That chapter first summarizes the events that took place in Egypt at the first Passover, when the lambs were killed, one for each household, and the angel of death passed over those Jewish families whose homes were marked by the blood of the innocent animal. The Passover was an illustration of the way in which God would later pass over those whose sins were covered by the death of Jesus Christ and deliver them from judgment. After this summary we read, "And it shall serve as a sign to you on your hand, and as a reminder on your forehead, that the law of the LORD may be in your mouth; for with a powerful hand the LORD brought you out of Egypt" (v. 9). The first great doctrine that they were to have before their eyes was the doctrine of the atonement, the doctrine of salvation through the shedding of blood.

The frontlets are mentioned a second time in Deuteronomy 6:4-8, which contains a summary of the character and requirements of God. "Hear, O Israel! The LORD is our God, the LORD is one! And you shall love the LORD your God with all your heart and with all your soul and with all your might. And these words, which I am commanding you today, shall be on your heart; and you shall teach them diligently to your sons and shall talk of them when you sit in your house and when you walk by the way and when you lie down and when you rise up. And you shall bind them as a sign on your hand and they shall be as frontals on your forehead." The second great doctrine to remember was the nature of God and man's corresponding responsibility to him. They were to love God with all their heart, and with all their soul, and with all their might.

The third mention of frontlets occurs five chapters later, in Deuteronomy 11:18. In this chapter God sets forth the principle by which He will bless the life of any individual or nation. The principle is obedience. Where there is obedience, God will give blessing. Where there is disobedience, He will send judgment. "You shall therefore impress these words of mine on your heart and on your soul; and you shall bind them as a sign on your hand, and they shall be as frontals on your forehead . . . so that your days and the days of your sons may be multiplied on the land which the LORD swore to your fathers to give them" (Deuteronomy 11:18, 21). The third great doctrine is the need for obedience, and it is to characterize our lives as God's people.

In this life neither you nor I will ever master all the great truths of Scripture. The Word of God is inexhaustible, like God Himself, and if our joy depended upon such a mastery, we would never actually experience it. But our joy does not depend on that. Our joy depends upon our relationship to God and our life with Him. However, if there is ever to be real joy in the Christian life, there must be a deep and growing experience of the basic truths upon which that life is founded. We must strive to know God better and to love Him. And we must attempt to live obediently before Him as His children.

There is a great deal of unrest in this world, and there will always be unrest for those who do not know Jesus. Apart from Him there is no true peace, no joy, and no real happiness either.

But that should never be the case for the Christian. If you are a Christian, you should draw close to God. You should feed on Scripture. And "the God of hope [will] fill you with all joy and peace in believing" (Romans 15:13).

13

How to Tell Others About Christ

When Jesus Christ told His disciples to "Go . . . and make disciples of all the nations, baptizing them in the name of the Father and the Son and the Holy Spirit" (Matthew 28:19), He was giving them what the Duke of Wellington once described as "marching orders for the church." They were to tell others about Him. They were to carry the gospel everywhere.

Unfortunately, it is entirely possible for you to understand that commission and even want to tell others about Christ, and yet still not know how. You might say, "I know what I should do, but how do I do it? How do I show that Jesus is the answer for the kid next door who is on drugs? How do I get my very sophisticated roommate to admit her need for Jesus Christ? How do I get the mechanic who works on my car to listen to my testimony? How do I overcome the built-in hostility toward the gospel by those who work with me every day? What words do I use to talk about Christ to my wife, my husband, my children, or my friends?"

If you have ever asked those questions, or are still asking them, then a study of the way in which Jesus related to the woman of

Samaria should be of help to you. As I look at Christ's dealings with the woman of Samaria, I see five great principles. I am convinced that if you learn from those principles and practice them, you will experience results similar to those of Christ's witness. For many of the Samaritans "went out of the city, and were coming to Him" (John 4:30).

The first principle is: *Be a friend* to those you are trying to win. Jesus showed Himself a friend to those who were lost. He has been described as a "friend of publicans and sinners." That (although intended critically) was quite accurate. Jesus could have kept aloof from mankind, but He would not have won anyone that way. Instead, Jesus came to the sick, lost, lonely, distressed, and perishing and moved among them as a friend. In this story we find Him in the woman's country, at the woman's city, sitting on the woman's well (John 4:5-6).

There is an illustration of this basic fact about the Lord Jesus in a book by Watchman Nee, the Christian evangelist. Nee had been talking to a friend in his home. They were downstairs, as was his friend's son. The friend's wife and mother were in an upstairs room. All at once the little boy wanted something and called out to his mother for it.

"It's up here," she said. "Come and get it."

He cried out to her, "I can't, Mummy; it's such a long way. Please bring it down to me."

He was very small. So the mother picked up what he wanted and brought it down to him. It is just that way with salvation. No one is able to meet his own need spiritually, but the Lord Jesus Christ came down to us so our need could be met. Nee writes, "Had He not come, sinners could not have approached Him; but He came down in order to lift them up."[1]

I wonder if you are like that in your witnessing? Do you keep aloof or do you go to those who need the gospel? Another way of asking the same thing is to ask whether or not you have contact with non-Christians socially. Do you go to their homes, sit in their kitchens, ask them their interests?

A great deal of our difficulty in this area comes from the fact that Christians often think the world will inevitably get them dirty if they come into contact with it. They take verses like 2 Corinthians 6:17—"THEREFORE, COME OUT FROM THEIR MIDST AND BE SEPARATE"—as meaning that Christians are to have no dealings with the world, rather than seeing that the verse only concerns avoiding conformity to the world, not withdrawal from it. Jesus did not teach isolation, and He did not practice it. He said in His great prayer for us, "I do not ask Thee to take them out of the world, but to keep them from the evil one" (John 17:15). When Christ departed for heaven He left His disciples *in the world* to evangelize it.

I am convinced that we need very practical ways of repeating Christ's obvious friendship with the lost in our personal experience. For a start you might invite a number of non-Christian friends into your home for dinner. You might go to a concert with them. You might take in a sports event. Why not befriend your co-workers? Join a club, a choral society, a civic organization. Go shopping together or invite your friends in for coffee. These are only beginning suggestions. If you are serious about taking the gospel to the lost, the Lord will show you other fruitful avenues of getting to know non-Christians. Just remember: Take the initiative and be friendly.

Second, *ask questions.* It is never a bad move to ask questions. As we read the story of Jesus' encounter with the Samaritan woman, we discover that that is precisely what He did at the very beginning of the conversation. He asked for a drink (v. 7). Looking at the conversation from the outside, as we do look at it, that is almost amusing. The woman was the one with the needs; she had the real questions. Jesus was the one with answers. Nevertheless, Jesus humbled Himself by asking a favor of her and so established an immediate and genuine point of contact.

Moreover, there were two very important consequences as the result of His asking the woman for something. First, He aroused her interest. Dale Carnegie reminds us in His successful book, *How to Win Friends and Influence People,* that the voice any person likes to hear best is his own. Jesus got the woman of

Samaria talking, which put her in a good mood—perhaps even changed her mood if she had arrived at the well shortly after being pushed off the path by Peter, as I believe could have been the case. Out of her good mood, the woman then clearly developed a favorable interest in Jesus. She must have found herself thinking, "My, what an interesting person this is! How polite! And what discrimination he must have to be interested in *me!*"

The second consequence was that the woman found her curiosity aroused. Jesus had asked her a question; she found it natural to begin to ask Him a series of questions. Here we should notice something quite interesting. In Jesus' conversation with Nicodemus, the first word Nicodemus is reported to have uttered is "How?" It was a question. The first word the woman of Samaria uttered was "How?" Again it was a question. No doubt there were many differences between the two questions. Perhaps there were even different motives in asking them. But the interesting point is that the two questions occurred. In those two instances where Jesus was witnessing to someone, He not only got the person talking, He got the person asking questions. He then answered them. We should do the same thing if we are to be effective in telling others about Christ.

Let me state this again in a slightly different way. People are always full of questions, many of them religious questions. If through your own questions you can get them to express their questions, by the grace of God you have already accomplished a great deal in your witness, and God will use the aroused interest to point the one asking the questions to Jesus. Paul Little has written correctly about provoking such questions: "Once the non-Christian takes the first step in initiative, all pressure goes out of any conversation about Jesus Christ." He adds that thereafter "it can be picked up at the point where it is left without embarrassment."[2]

Third, *offer something relevant*. Jesus offered the woman something related quite directly to her need. In one sense the offer was always of Himself, of course. Yet to aging Nicodemus

Jesus spoke of Himself as one who offers new life, a new beginning (John 3:3). To the man who had been born blind He spoke of Himself as light (John 9:5). To the woman the same offer was couched in the metaphor of water. He said, "Whoever drinks of the water that I shall give him shall never thirst; but the water that I shall give him shall become in him a well of water springing up to eternal life" (John 4:14).

Most Christians need to learn from this principle. It will not do for us to witness about the transmission and reliability of the Bible if we are talking to a girl who is not interested in that but is afraid she will end up an old maid if she becomes a Christian. We must share Christ's offer to guide our lives and enrich them in whatever way He leads us.

It will not be much use for us to speak about the power of Jesus Christ being able to deliver a person from the grip of drugs or alcohol if we are speaking to a disciplined scientist whose greatest hangup is his suspicion that other scientists have disproved Christianity. We need to offer him the challenge of searching the Scriptures himself to see whether those things are so and to encourage him to test Christ's claims. Above all, we must not present our message in the language of the last century or in clichés that have no meaning to most of the non-Christian world.

Most people are thinking of their own needs. We must offer Jesus to them in ways that relate to those needs.

Fourth, *stress the good news*. Show that the gospel of Jesus Christ offers comfort. I am sure you realize that that does not mean we are totally to overlook sin. Jesus did not do that. He brought the woman to the point of recognizing her sin by His reference to the issue of her husbands. Nevertheless, even as He gently uncovered the sin, He offered comfort; for He coupled His inquiry into her marital status with the invitation to come again to Him (John 4:16).

Unfortunately, it is true that we often do exactly the opposite in witnessing to non-Christians. The comfort of the gospel is there, but we forget the comfort in our zeal to expose (and, I am afraid, often condemn) the sin. For instance, imagine a situation in which a non-Christian offers a Christian a drink at a party. Aren't there thousands of Christians who would immediately reply, "No, thank you. I don't drink. I'm a Christian." They then think they have offered a splendid witness to Jesus Christ when actually they have only succeeded in condemning the non-Christian. At the same time they would give him the wrong idea that non-drinking is somehow a very important part of Christianity. Non-drinking may be an important part of their Christian life. But the point I am making is that the statement, "I don't drink. I'm a Christian," is no more intelligible to the non-Christian than it would be for him to say, when you ask him to go to a football game, "No, thanks. I don't go to football games. I'm a non-Christian."

There are two real dangers in all of this. The first is the danger that in getting our witness tangled up in such issues we miss the fact that our friend may be quite desperately lonely—perhaps that is why he drinks—and we never suggest a cure for his loneliness. Or we may miss his feeling of guilt, sorrow, meaninglessness, or whatever it may be.

The second danger is that in focusing attention on some aspect of the nonbeliever's conduct we may actually give the impression that he must improve himself before he can come to Jesus. That is quite wrong. We never want to give the impression that, when we come to Jesus, we can do as we please, that we can sin that grace might abound. That also would be untrue. But neither do we want to suggest that there must be self-reformation before a man or woman can come.

In England, in the early part of the nineteenth century, there was a woman who had heard the gospel but had never been able to respond to it personally. She had come from a Christian home. She understood the faith. But still she could not come. She considered herself unworthy. One day she wandered into a very small church and sat down in the back. She was almost in despair and hardly heard the words of the elderly man who was speaking. Suddenly, right in the middle of his address, the

How to Tell Others About Christ

preacher stopped and pointing his finger at her said, "You, Miss, sitting there at the back, you can be saved *now*. You don't need to do anything!" His words struck like thunder in her heart. She believed at once, and with her belief there came an unimaginable sense of peace and real joy. That night Charlotte Elliott went home and wrote the well-known hymn:

> Just as I am, without one plea,
> But that thy blood was shed for me,
> And that thou bidd'st me come to thee,
> O Lamb of God, I come! I come!

If we are to witness for Jesus Christ, we must never give the impression that a man must first become worthy of the gospel. We must not forget that there is comfort in the gospel for sinners.

The fifth principle is that we must end by confronting the individual with his *responsibility to decide* for or against Jesus Christ. Jesus said, "I . . . am He [the Messiah]" (John 4:26). Well, was He or wasn't He? That was the decision placed before the woman. It must be the same in our witnessing. If we do not get to the point of focusing on Jesus Himself, our witness is incomplete. And if we do not get to the point of showing that a decision is necessary, our witness is inadequate.

These are the principles of how we should tell others about Jesus Christ, taken from the story of Jesus' encounter with the Samaritan woman. First, be friendly. Second, ask questions. Third, offer that which most suits the individual's needs. Fourth, stress the good news. And fifth, show that the person must decide either for or against the Lord Jesus Christ.

What will happen if you do that? I believe that the results will be similar to those that Jesus experienced in Samaria. The first obvious results were in the life of the woman. About midway through the conversation the woman acknowledged her need, saying, "Give me this water, so I will not be thirsty" (John 4:15). A few moments later she confessed her sin, "I have no husband" (v. 17). Then she began to show a quickening of spiritual intelligence: "I perceive that You are a prophet" (v. 19). Next she affirmed her faith in Jesus: "Is not this the Christ?" (v. 29, KJV). Finally, she took to others the good news that she had received.

You may think the people among whom you work or with whom you associate are difficult specimens to speak to. That may be true. So was the woman. And yet she became the first great witness after John the Baptist. It may be that God will use your witness to reach one who in turn may evangelize an entire generation.

Notes

1. Watchman Nee, *What Shall This Man Do?* (London: Victory, 1962), p. 37.
2. Paul E. Little, *How to Give Away Your Faith* (Downers Grove, Ill.: Inter-Varsity, 1966), p. 36.

Scripture Index

Genesis		**Isaiah**		4:15	111
1:27	58	28:10	72	4:16	109
1:28	58			4:17	111
2:18	58	**Matthew**		4:19	112
2:22	58	4	81	4:23-24	26
2:24	58, 59	4:1-11	80	4:26	111
3:16	66	4:3-4	82	4:29	112
		4:7	82	4:30	106
Exodus		4:10	82	6:39-40	37
13	102	5:21-22	84	7:17	35
13:9	102	5:23-24	85	9:5	109
20:12	71	5:48	11	13:24	92
20:13	83	6:5-8	18	14:6	20, 31
40:36-37	36	6:7-8	23	14:9	34
		6:9	79	15:3	80
Numbers		6:13	79	15:10-11	102
35:30	83	6:19-21	93	15:11	98
		6:24	91	17:13	98
Deuteronomy		6:25	91	17:15	107
6:4-8	102	6:25, 32-33	90	17:17	30
6:13	82	6:26-30	91	18:10	93
6:16	82	6:26, 28-30	92		
8:3	82	6:31	91	**Acts**	
11:18	103	6:32, 33	91	15:10-11	46
11:21	103	6:33	93		
		6:34	91	**Romans**	
1 Samuel		11:28-30	94	1:20	34
15:22	86	14:30	92	3:23	10
		15:8-9	30	5:8	14
2 Chronicles		16:22	93	6:14	45
8:11	62	17:24-27	92	6:15	46
		19:4-9	58	6:22	46
Psalms		28:19	105	8:7	35
19:8	101			8:26-27	22
32:8	39	**Luke**		12:1, 2	37, 79
66:18	22, 86	2:10-11	98	12:2	55, 87
119:9, 11	80			12:19-21	88
119:14	101	**John**		14:17	101
		3:3	109	15:13	104
Proverbs		3:7	26		
6:20-21	71	3:14	26	**1 Corinthians**	
13:24	71	3:16	14	1:30	15
19:18	71	4:5-6	113	6:12	45, 47, 15
22:15	71	4:7	107	6:13-20	47
23:13	71	4:14	109	6:18	77, 79

8:13	49	5:26-28	70	2 TIMOTHY	
10:13	82	5:32	63	2:22	77, 79
10:23	45, 48	6:1	65		
11:3	67	6:5-6	38	HEBREWS	
		6:17	80	2:17-18	76
2 CORINTHIANS				4:15	80
6:14	63	PHILIPPIANS		10:19, 22	20
6:17	107	2:5	52	12:14-15	87
		2:15	54		
GALATIANS		3:3	26	JAMES	
2:11-14	46	4:1-4	55	1:2-3	76
5	26, 54	4:2	54	1:13-14	76
5:22-23	98	4:2-5	52	1:27	76
		4:4	53	4:7	76, 79
EPHESIANS		4:5	54		
2:18	22	4:6	90	1 PETER	
4:26	87	4:6-7	101	3:1	66
5	69	4:8	38, 45, 49, 50	3:7	70
5:4	66	4:9	50	5:7	91, 93
5:21	67				
5:22	63	COLOSSIANS		1 JOHN	
5:22-24	66	3:18	66	3:18, 20	86
5:22-30	65	3:23	38	3:22	23
5:25	63				

Subject Index

ABC's of salvation, 9
Abraham, 76
Adam, 62, 81
Alcohol, 44, 78
Anxiety, 89-90, 101
Ark of the Covenant, 31
Atonement, the, 102
  day of, 31
Auca Indians, 44

Barclay, William, 28
Barnhouse, Donald Grey, 34, 58
Barrett, Ethel, 48
Barth, Karl, 25
Bathsheba, 77
Belief, 16, 111. See also Faith, Trust
Bernard of Clairvaux, 32
Bible. See Word of God
Bible Study Hour, 7, 80

Calvin, John, 30
Canaan, 37
Capone, Al, 13
Carnegie, Dale, 107
Chastisement. See Discipline
Chaucer, Geoffrey, 27
Christ Jesus, able to save, 93
  and the church, 63-65, 68-69
  asked questions, 107-108
  commitment to, 9, 15-16, 18, 44, 100
  cross of, 31, 100
  death of, 10, 14, 16, 21, 31, 86, 94, 102
  faith in, 21, 62, 100, 112
  fellowship with, 31
  friend of the lost, 106-107
  guidance by, 109
  humility of, 107
  love of, 16, 63, 69
  meets our needs, 108-109
  methods of witnessing, 105-112
  our example, 81
  promises of, 93-94, 97-98
  removed sin, 14
  resurrection of, 94
  revelation of God, 34
  righteousness of, 14
  Savior, 10, 16, 21
  teaching of, 18, 22, 35, 58, 90-94
  temptation of, 79-80
  way to God, 9, 30
  without sin, 16, 76, 80
Christian, and doubtful things, 43, 50
  becoming a, 9-16
  a child of God, 100-101
  clothed in righteousness, 14, 16
  marriage, 57-64
  new nature of a, 26
  spirit of a, 27-29
  surrendered, 55
Christian life, 100
  contact with unbelievers, 106
  dealing with worry, 89-95
  fruit of, 98, 100
  growth in the, 31, 37, 47
  obedience a part of, 37, 103
  overcoming anger, 83-88
  temptations of the, 75-82
  warfare of the, 52, 79
  witnessing, 105-111
Christianity, 43
  defined, 11
  the upward way, 8
Christians, a new creation, 73
  at Rome, 54
  citizens of heaven, 14
  conformed to Christ, 14
  duty of, 76
  families of, 55, 65-73
  formerly aliens, 14
  getting along with others, 51-55
  God's people, 14
  Jewish, 45
  joy of, 53, 97-102
  knowing the will of God, 23, 33-50, 103
  living for others, 47

rejoicing, 53-54
saved from sin, 90
taboos of, 43
transformation of, 14, 79, 87-88
unity of, 53, 55, 61-62
Church, at Philippi, 51
liturgy of the, 28
medieval, 30
of England, 29
of the first century, 45
of the living God, 30
Clothing, 44, 48
Cloud in the desert, 35-37
Commandments, of God, 23, 37, 92, 102
of men, 30
Commitment to Jesus Christ, 9, 15-16, 18, 44, 100
Conduct, 48, 52, 54, 110. See also Standards
Confession, 21-22
Creation, 34

Dating, 72
David, 22, 62, 77, 86
Day of Atonement, 31
Devil. See Satan
Discipline, 71-72
Disobedience, 62, 71, 86, 103
Divorce, 58, 60, 81
Doctrine of Scripture, 30, 54, 101-102
Doubtful things, 43-50
Duke of Wellington, 105

Egypt, 35, 62, 102
Elliot, Elizabeth, 44
Elliot, Jim, 44
Elliott, Charlotte, 111
Euodia, 51-52
Eve, 81

Faith, in Christ Jesus, 20, 62, 100, 111
in God, 89
strengthened, 76, 94
Fall, the, 81
Families, 55
duty of children, 65, 71-73
duty of parents, 66, 71-73
Fellowship, with Christ, 31
with God, 14, 39, 49, 52, 103

Flesh, 59
sins of, 77-78
Food, 47, 78, 82
Freedom, 48-49, 89-95
from guilt, 21

God, acceptance by, 15
access to, 19, 30-32
answers prayer, 17, 19, 22
attributes of, 28
care of, 91-95
commandments of, 23, 37, 92, 102
creativity of, 40
demands of, 13, 15
far away, 22
fellowship with, 14, 39, 49, 52, 103
gift of, 14, 47, 70
glory to, 24
goodness of, 53, 97-98
grace of, 47, 62-64, 97
guidance of, 33
helper in temptation, 75
holy, 10, 20
inexhaustible, 103
Lamb of, 31
looking to, 22
love of, 9
name of, 24
nature of, 21, 27, 34, 54, 94, 103
obedience to, 37
people of, 14
prayers to, 19-20
presence of, 14, 19, 21-23, 31, 35, 50
promises of, 50, 62, 88, 94, 100
purposes in marriage, 57-64
requirements of, 10-11, 13-14, 37, 100, 102
revelation of, 23, 34
righteousness of, 11, 13-15, 100
source of joy, 98, 101, 103
sovereignty of, 17
standards of, 11, 100, 111
stronger than Satan, 79
will of, 23, 33-50, 62, 79-80, 101
wants men to believe, 10, 13
worship of, 25-32, 82
Goodness, of God, 53, 97-98
of man, 11, 13-14, 21
Gospel, 55, 100, 106, 109, 111

Subject Index

Grace, 45-46
　of God, 47, 61, 63, 97, 108
　standing in, 16
Graham, Billy, 70, 72
Greek ethics, 49
Guidance, 18, 33, 109
Guilt, 21, 63, 84, 110

Habits, 47, 94
Happiness, 46, 51, 54, 98, 101, 103
　as a family, 65-73
　in marriage, 57-64
Heart, 12-13, 15, 20, 30, 84-85, 87-88, 103
Heaven, 14, 82, 86, 88, 107
Holiness, life of, 38, 46, 101
　of God, 10, 20-21
Holy Spirit, 22, 55, 62, 78, 101
　evidence of, 26
　fruit of, 53-54
　work of, 27
Holy of Holies, 31
Holy Place, 31
Human goodness, 11, 13, 15, 21

Isaac, 76
Israel, 45, 83
Israelites, 35

Jerusalem, 28, 46, 62, 81-82, 86
Jesus Christ. *See* Christ Jesus
Jews, 45, 102
John the Baptist, 112
John the Evangelist, 23
Joseph, 78
Joy, 15, 21, 53-54, 97-103, 111

Kierkegaard, Soren, 90

Lamont, Robert, 66
Law, 14, 46-47, 58
Law and grace, 45-46
Lewis, C. S., 15, 29, 59
Liberty, 46, 49
License, 46
Little, Paul, 108
Lord's Prayer, 18, 79
Love, for God, 103
　of Christ, 16, 64, 68-69
　of God, 9, 14
　of a husband for his wife, 63, 66-67, 69, 72

　of money, 91
　rather than law, 46-47
　rather than passion, 98
　romantic, 59
Luther, Martin, 16, 23, 30

Maier, Walter D., 58
Man, commandments of, 29
　nature of, 28
　purpose of, 32
　responsibility to God, 103
　soul of, 59
　spiritual blindness of, 13, 35
　a trinity, 59
Marriage, 47, 101
　Christian, 61
　courtship preceding, 72
　duties of husband, 65-71
　duties of wife, 65-69
　happiness in, 57-64
　true, 61
　types of, 46-47
　union in, 47, 58-61
Mass, the Catholic, 30
Mercy seat, 31
Miller, Keith, 61, 70
Mind, 12, 22, 35, 61, 79, 85, 87
　of Christ, 52
Money, 91
Moses, 31
Mount Gerizim, 28
Myconius, Frederick, 23

Nee, Watchman, 106
Nicodemus, 108

Obedience, 37, 67, 71, 86, 103. *See also* Submission

Pagan morality, 49
Passover, 102
Paul, 14, 34, 45, 51-52
Peter, 45, 92, 108
Pharisee, 14
Pillar of fire, 35
Prayer, 16, 31, 41, 76, 79, 81-82, 86, 97, 107
　answered, 23, 92
　basis of, 20
　boldness in, 23
　defined, 17, 20
　hindered by sin, 21-22

means of access, 19
methods of, 17-24
offered to God, 19-20
privilege, 20
public, 18
purpose of, 17
questions about, 17-20
restrictions on, 18-19
to idols, 19
to men, 19
to saints, 19
with family, 71-72
with others, 18
work of Holy Spirit, 22
Promises, of Christ, 93-94, 97-98
of God, 62, 94
Protestant Reformation, 30, 34

Revelation, 23
Righteousness, clothed in, 14, 16
external, 12
from God, 16, 21
of God, 11, 13-15, 100
of law, 14
of man, 11-15
thirst after, 93

Salvation, 9, 14, 30, 52, 87, 94, 98, 106
Samuel, 86
Satan, 76, 79-82
Saul, 86
Scripture. See Word of God
Sermon on the Mount, 11, 23-27, 80, 90, 93-94
Sex, 47, 59-60
Sexual sins, 48, 77-78
Shakespeare, William, 27
Sin, 54, 77-78, 92, 100, 102, 109
clothed in, 14
confessed, 21-22, 31, 85-86
consequences, 86
free from, 47
hinders prayer, 22
must be punished, 14
removed by Christ, 9, 14
unconfessed, 86
Sinful nature, 81
Solomon, 62
Standards, 44, 48-49, 54, 61, 69, 72-73, 108-109. See also Conduct

Submission, defined, 79
of women to their husbands, 66-68, 72
to God, 86-87, 100
Suffering, triumph in, 97-104
Syntyche, 51-52

Tabernacle, design of, 31
significance of, 31
Teas, Walt, 80
Temple in Jerusalem, 28, 62, 81-82, 86
Temple, Samaritan, 28
Temptation, defined, 76
from the devil, 76-77, 79
from the flesh, 75-77, 80-81
from the world, 76-77, 80-81
how to defeat, 75-82
of Jesus Christ, 80-82
solution to, 77-81
two kinds of, 76-77
Temptations, from God, 76-77
not from God, 76-77
Testing, 76
Timothy, 77
Titedios Amerimnos, 95
Triumph in suffering, 97-104
Trust, 15, 76, 82, 92, 101. See also Faith, Belief
Torrey, Reuben A., 20

Unbelievers, 37, 62, 106, 109-110
Union in marriage, 47, 58-61
Unity among Christians, 53, 55, 60-61

Values, 49-50, 78
Virtues, 49, 53

Walking with God, 52, 62
Warfare, 52, 79-80
Westminster Shorter Catechism, 32, 34, 91
Wilde, Oscar, 75
Wilkerson, David, 40
Will of God, 62, 79-80, 101
for unbelievers, 37
how to know the, 23, 33-50
Witnessing, dangers in, 110
how to go about, 105-112
Woman of Samaria, 27-28, 105-112
Women, 44, 66-69, 72

Subject Index

Word of God, 30, 37, 77, 80, 82, 99, 103
  authority of, 63
  doctrine of, 30, 54, 101-102
  principles of, 45-49, 101-102
  revelation of, 23, 34
  solution to worry in, 89-90
  study of, 71, 80, 86, 101-103
  teaching of, 10
Word Studies, "care," 93
  "happiness," 98
  "prosagoge," 22
  "reasonableness," 54
  "rejoice," 53
World, 82, 98, 103, 107
  source of temptation, 76-78
Worry, 89-90, 101
  freedom from, 89-95
  hinders prayer, 22
Worship, defined, 27
  evidence of a new nature, 26
  false, 28
  how to, 25-32
  liturgy used, 28-29
  of God, 82
  of Satan, 81-82
  origin of, 28
  place of, 27-28
  true, 28-29
  with family, 71

Moody Press, a ministry of the Moody Bible Institute, is designed for education, evangelization and edification. If we may assist you in knowing more about Christ and the Christian life, please write us without obligation to: Moody Press, c/o MLM, Chicago, Illinois 60610.